The Symphony of High Dimensional Wisdoms

By Mr. Liu Feng

Translated by Bo Ai

Absolute Author
Publishing House

The Symphony of High Dimensional Wisdoms
Copyright © 2021 Feng Liu
All Rights Reserved

Translator: Bo Ai
Publishing Editor: Dr. Melissa Caudle, USA
Editor: Margaret Mee
Paperback ISBN: 978-1-64953-169-8
eBook ISBN: 978-1-64953-170-4
Sponsored By: International Holographic Ecology Ltd

INTERNATIONAL
IHE HOLOGRAPHIC
ECOLOGY

Website: www.ihe.org.au
Contact: info@ihe.org.au

(Scan this code with Wechat APP)

ABOUT THE AUTHOR

MR. LIU FENG

- Public speaker and disseminator of the Holistic Universe Theory
- Chairman of the Advisory Committee of Beijing Shifangyuan Elderly Hospice and Mind Care Center
- Chief Expert of the America Holographic Institute of Life Sciences
- Chief Expert of the International Holographic Ecology LTD
- The Author of the Best-Selling book Open Your High-Dimensional Wisdom (Language: Chinese)

During his 30 years of research study and application on the subject of General Space-time Energy, Mr. Liu Feng has dedicated himself to both the theoretical study and experiential exploration of all kinds of Sapience Methods & Spiritual Groups with a total open mind. He interacts harmoniously with today's pluralistic world, with a basic Principle of "Seeking the Common and Respect the Difference". Mr. Liu has unscrambled and interpreted various mankind wisdom systems with a scientific logic, by which people with different backgrounds have been greatly inspired.

Mr. Liu Feng is also an expert in corporation management with a seven-year top managerial experience in a high-tech company (Oplink Co. at Silicon Valley). He had been through the whole process in the company from its very beginning to its IPO. He has also been a high-tech industrial consultant (President GOC, a managerial consultancy company) for more than six years. He led several high-tech companies and launched manufacturing plants in China. Mr. Liu Feng has been an architect of corporate culture for many enterprises and helped them adapt to future-oriented culture based on the combination of Eastern and Western wisdom.

PRAISE

This book is the common intellectual wealth of mankind, an internal bridge which connects each entity and the organization, a hub connecting all wisdom systems in our human society; and is the shared basic frequency in the harmonious symphony of multiculturalism in our society. I am grateful to the inner "self" for creating this opportunity, the yuan, to meet with you through the development of this book. Those who benefit the most will be those who participate. This is the common experience shared by practitioners of Xin Neng Yuan. **- Mr. Liu Feng**

More than ten years ago, I saw Mr. Liu Feng's lectures on High Dimensional Wisdoms. In 2019, I came across a video of Mr. Liu Feng lecturing on "Infinite Light and Infinite Life", and it struck a chord in my heart. I felt that lecture was specifically addressed to me. His meaningful words were a sound theoretical summary of what I had been practicing over the past 20 years. I wish this book to be a success, and more and more people will have the opportunity to benefit from Mr. Liu's teachings. **- Yisheng Zhao, Principal, Perth I Ching Academy**

In this world full of materialism, many people lose their way, do not understand the meaning of life, let alone the value of life. Sometimes I felt lonely. When I met Mr. Liu Feng, his research on the high-dimensional wisdom of the universe suddenly penetrated my heart and made my life full of strength. I was at ease in my life, believing in perfection, and no longer lonely. Do appreciate this opportunity to meet Mr. Liu Feng in your life. **– Pei Guo**

The awareness dimension, level, disposition and breadth of Mr. Liu Feng have all had a profound impact on my life. What is particularly precious to individuals and groups alike is the important direction provided by Mr. Liu Feng in his 30 years of multicultural system compilation in the realm of inner growth groups. This book has afforded me tremendous help in the dimension of how scientific context can uplift awareness energy, and I will keep on studying it. **- Songlin Liu, Founder of Bene Wellness, Initiator of Holistic Wellness International Forum with Holistic Center Networks**

I made Mr. Liu Feng's acquaintance ten years ago, and we co-founded the "Shi-Fang-Yuan" elderly mental care charity organisation, providing mental care services for 40 million severely ill, terminal-stage elderly in China. Mr. Liu Feng's theory system has made an impact on the life satisfaction of thousands of people. I look forward to the publication of the English version of the book "Tapping into Higher-Dimension Wisdom". I believe it will connect with more people who are meant to be, and awaken the satisfaction originating from life. **- Shugong Fang, Director, Beijing Shi-Fang-Yuan Elderly Mental Care Centre, Secretary-General of the Beijing Shi-Fang-Yuan Charity Foundation, Executive Director of China Life Care Association**

Since the breakout of the COVID-19 pandemic in the beginning of 2020, we have seen the relationship between the community with a shared future for mankind and each person, and that no single nation, people, or individual can remain unaffected in this day and age. Mr. Liu Feng has spent 30 years seeking the common components in all of the wisdom systems he has had the fortune to come into contact with and forming this wisdom system of the fundamental principles of the universe. For this wisdom system, Mr. Liu Feng has not invented any peculiar names or terminologies, but has only borrowed from the universal and simplest scientific terms and logics, for the purpose of revealing the meaning of life to each being from the perspective of now. **- Liwei Wang**

Table of Contents

Mr. Liu Feng

Lecture 1 The Principle of the Ultimate Simplicity of the Universe

An Expedient Context for Linking all Human Wisdom Systems

I'd like to explain the overarching principle of my lectures. I'd like to name it "To Seek Commonality and Respect Differences." This term differs from the usual saying, which goes, "To Seek Commonality and Reserve Differences." These two sayings are different as the latter expresses objectivity but maintains the narrator's position. The narrator of the former expression is not clinging to a position but rather respecting the reasonable existence of all things in time and space. In fact, in the past thirty years, when I explored a wisdom system, for example, a religion, or a practice method, I held this saying as my overarching principle.

When I explored all the wisdom systems, I tried to find and verify the commonalities among them, as mentioned above.

The Symphony of High Dimensional Wisdoms

When I respected the reasonable existence of all things in time and space and appreciated each system's unique characteristics, I could find the genuine beauty in the commonalities among them. And this process was a process full of joy and happiness. Therefore, today, after many years of experience and after combing through all the wisdom systems, I am going to share with you the essence.

Today, I'll start with the first lecture that I presented. The title is "The Principle of Ultimate Simplicity of The Universe." The subtitle is "An Expedient Context for Linking All Human Wisdom Systems". Why do I name it "The Principle of Ultimate Simplicity of The Universe?" In the universe we are in now, there are endless systems defining wisdom, and more descriptions are emerging all the time. When one inwardly seeks to see his own heart and mind and cultivates to a certain level, he realizes a lot of information that could not be realized in a three-dimensional world—our usual environment, higher-dimensional descriptions are multifaceted. Anyone could create a system, and each of the creators will face one problem—the problem of making his system known to others. New names and new terms need to be interpreted to ensure an obstacle-free understanding of the new system. The biggest problem among all these wisdom systems is their effective communication. Each wisdom system deems it has found the truth, and the followers of each wisdom system believe they have received great inspirations from the truth. In our world today, where we could see many wisdom systems moving forward in their pursuit, communication and mutual verification among these wisdom systems become essential. Otherwise, one would feel confused. When different language contexts meet, even though the same topic is being discussed, one would feel confused because of the adoption of varying logic, names, and terms.

Of all the wisdom systems, the most universally applicable system in our modern world is the scientific context. Scientific context is a logic system collectively summarized from the development of new knowledge in the past few hundred years. It has no connotation concerning ethnicity, nationality, politics, or religion. Why don't I name it just science? If I were to call it science, many paradoxes would appear, as different people have different views on science. There are relative limitations in the description of science in the public knowledge system domain. Therefore, I name it a scientific context, and I only want to borrow scientific names, terms, and logical relationships because the public widely accepts them. For example, when I write "$1 + 1 = $ on the ground," almost everyone in the world will write "2."

Every system also has its complexity. When I looked for the commonalities, I found that commonalities are really clear. However, when trying to link up each system's simplicity to the simplicity, or complexity, of another system, it is rather tricky. Therefore, to explore the descriptions among different systems and verify them, and truly comprehend their core commonalities, is our lectures.

Now let's discuss part one, The Concept of Multi-Dimensional Space.

The Symphony of High Dimensional Wisdoms

There are many systems for describing space in the scientific context. For example, there is the rectangular coordinate system, linear geometric systems; and there is the spherical coordinate system, polar coordinate system, binary system, etc. Among these systems that describe the existence of space, there are formulas, or interfaces, for connections. However, I choose only the rectangular coordinate system, also known as the linear geometric system.

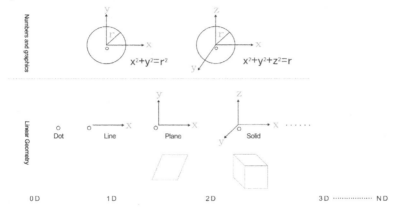

Figure 1 Rectangular system and multidimensional concept

Why do I choose this system? Because of all systems, this is the closest to our daily experience. When most of us studied mathematics, we understood this system.

The multi-dimensional space system is a system that starts with the 0th dimension, and it extends to the Nth dimensions (N approaches infinity). From a Mass Point to the Nth dimensions (N approaches infinity), the rectangular coordinate system is a good way for describing the entire universe. Nothing, no information or matter, could be out of its coverage.

5

In more detail, the 0 dimension is a Mass Point, a particle; the single dimension is a straight line; the two dimensions form a plane, and the three dimensions create a space. In the 0 dimensions, there is no variable. It is just a Mass Point in space.

There is one variable in a single dimension, which, in mathematics, is often replaced with X. We called it the X-axis. Four arithmetic operations are performed on this axis: addition, subtraction, multiplication, and division.

The two dimensions form a plane that has two variables, X and Y. In three-dimensional space, there are three variables, X, Y, and Z. This concept is familiar to most of us. When I talked to my friends about this concept twenty or thirty years ago, they found it hard to understand. Today, the term "multi-dimensional space" can be seen in many places-- from psychology, crypto-psychism to modern culture, art, movies, and games. It is convenient for our discussions.

The one, two, and three dimensions in mathematics correspond strictly to those in physics. This means nearly all physic questions ended up abstractly as mathematical problems. Mathematics describes the relationship between numbers and forms. In the three-dimensional world, there is a strict correspondence between number and form. In our world, all activities could be summarized into a Characteristic Equation, a mathematical model. When we study computer programming, there is a word called "modelling" --that is, finding the mathematical model within one subject. Find the model and then describe it. In three-dimensional space, we could discover endless proofs.

However, most people could not find any evidence in four-dimensional space. Maybe one would say four-dimensional space doesn't even exist. There is another explanation.

Equipped, as most of us are, with three-dimensional cognitive and sensual capabilities, we are restricted by these abilities, just as an ant, an insect with only two-dimensional capabilities, is limited to the two-dimensional plane. When we use chalk and draw an ant surrounded by a circle, there is no way for the ant to break away from this sealed, two-dimensional enclosure. We human beings have three-dimensional cognitive and sensual capabilities. When we are restricted by or are confined within a three-dimensional space, we cannot leave the sealed, three-dimensional enclosure, either. However, a being from a higher-dimensional space could take objects from the closed, three-dimensional enclosure. Even though this may sound supernatural, the theoretical logic is very sound. Why? Because with an increase in a dimension, there is one more variable. The mathematical theories behind all the operations never change. We know that there is only one variable on the number axis when doing arithmetic. Where algebra is concerned, we adopt one special method-- Formula Subtraction--when we need to interpret two variables. What is Formula Subtraction? It is the dimension lowering that turns a two-dimensional problem into a single-dimensional one.

Through the comparative study of the three dimensions, we understand its precision. To continue the exploration, we search for the verification process in the higher dimensions. In a mathematical system, all dimensions, from zero to N (N approaches infinity), exist. If this is a logical assumption, there is no reason that this assumption only exists in up to three dimensions. Most of us could not verify higher dimensions because most of us only have three-dimensional cognitive and sensual capabilities. You cannot break through three-dimensional space through three-dimensional activities.

Human beings have been continually breaking through the way we think and expanding our limitations in the past centuries throughout our modern science development. However, we have been confined to our deep-rooted way of practice. We have been relying on eyes, ears, nose, tongue, and body to understand the universe; therefore, we have confined ourselves to a very narrow three-dimensional space. When the scientific domain of definition extended from three-dimensional space to N-dimensional space (N approaches infinity), we realized the vastness and possibility of mutual understanding among the universe's wisdom systems. The most prevalent misunderstanding we still have is trying to solve high-dimensional problems in a three-dimensional mind-set. Logically, this is quite ridiculous.

"Practice is the sole criterion for testing truth", a well-known saying by Chairman Mao. Yet, three-dimensional practice is the sole criterion for testing truth in three-dimensional space, and high-dimensional practice is the sole criterion for testing truth in high-dimensional spaces. It is impossible for people living in three-dimensional space to test the truth in higher dimensional space, just as an ant could not test the truth in the world of human beings.

Therefore, truly valuable practices are those that can be practiced in all spaces. The space we are talking about is a space ranging from zero to N (N approaches infinity) dimensions.

What are the differences between each space? In a one-dimensional world, there is an infinite number of points; in a two-dimensional world, there is an infinite number of lines; in a three-dimensional world, there is an infinite number of planes. From these we could summarize a very simple concept, namely, with the addition of one dimension, there will be infinitely times more information, and correlations. This reveals one important possibility: with the increase of one additional dimension, there will be an infinite number more wisdoms of the universe. This could help us understand the differences in the descriptions of different wisdom systems in our world, as well as the huge differences between the current situations of human beings and those of the highest realm.

Now let's talk about what exists in a space. To describe existence, we use a remarkably simple way. We called it "to search for commonality." All the beings we see in a three-dimensional world are already too complicated. It is impossible for us to fully understand all existences in the material world in one's lifetime, let alone in the information age that we are now entering, in which even broader forms of existence are included. Happily, the search for commonality among material things can be accomplished by a relatively simple line of inquiry.

To begin, we know that the commonality of all existence is the molecule. It is molecules that form all matter. To explore further, the commonality of molecules is an atom.

Atoms form a molecule. An atom is composed of a nucleus and one or more electrons. Nuclei differ, and the electron is the commonality. A nucleus is composed of one or more protons and several neutrons, which is the commonality. A proton is composed of neutrons and positron (positive electrons).

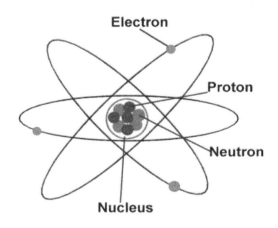

Figure 2 Atomic Structure

Thus, we find that all tangible matter is composed of three elementary forms of existence: neutron, positron, and negative electron. This could be regarded as corresponding to "three produces all things", as the Dao De Jing (道德经) has described it. These three particles are referred to as the three most elementary particles. The commonality among these three particles is the quantum property in the field of modern physics. The quantum property is the wave-particle duality. The commonality of the wave-particle duality is the energy wave. In other words, wave is the commonality of the wave-particle duality. So, what is the nature of a particle? From the Light Wave Theory and the Theory of Wave Interference, we understand that the nature of a particle is interferometric imaging. Modern scientific research of electrons found that they are actually not physical particles but wave packets. A wave packet is a short burst or envelope of localized wave action that travels as a unit. We also use the term "standing wave" to describe it. In other words, it is the relatively stable interferometric imaging of a wave in the space.

Now we know when the wave forms the interferometric imaging of a standing wave in space, we can see its existence. This is called "particle nature". In Buddhist scriptures, when describing the initial existence of this universe, the term "se" (色) or form, is used. With the interference of a wave in action, interferometric imaging is formed, namely the nature of particles is visible. When the condition for the interference is not available, when there is no space phase to interfere with the standing wave, even with the presence of energy, or an energy wave, the imaging would not be visible. This, in the Buddhist scriptures, is called "void" (空), or emptiness. Hence, often we see the text, "Form is emptiness, emptiness is form; emptiness is no other than form, form too is no other than emptiness." Further, "they are not defiled, they are not undefiled; they

are not deficient, and they are not complete".

Now we have found the real commonality among all existence. We have covered energy waves already, and there are actually many types of energy waves. There are

11

square waves, rectangular waves, triangle waves etc. and various complex waveforms. What is their commonality? Through Fourier Equation, we know that all complex energy waves and waveforms can be disassembled and decomposed, and eventually, the essence is the sine wave, sin X. Now we find that the sine wave is the real commonality. More interestingly, there is another name for the sine wave–a simple harmonic wave. In the traditional culture, there is a saying, called "Da Dao Zhi Jian", the Great Way is the Ultimate Simple One. Therefore, the simplest commonality of this universe is a sine wave.

What is a sine wave called in the Buddhist scriptures? Thought - to give rise to a thought. In Buddhism, we say, "One thought is one being." According to the Buddhist doctrines, when we try to understand the universe's existence, we learn that it is a congregation of beings. And every single being results from a thought.

In Daoism, the sine wave is called Tai Ji, which has two parts, the Yin and the Yang. There are two parts to a sine wave. The upper part is the Yang, the positive, and the lower part is the Yin, the negative.

In information technology, we call it Unit Information, which is also a sine wave. The amplitude, the wavelength, or the frequency, and its position and phase in space, form an information unit, which is the most basic information, a sine wave. In traditional Chinese culture, the image of a dragon resembles the shape of sine waves. Therefore, when we say we are descendants of a dragon, it is very scientific because all existence comes from the sine way, namely, from the dragon.

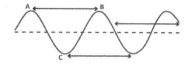

Sine Wave is the fundamental
existence in the universe.

Information unit a+b=1

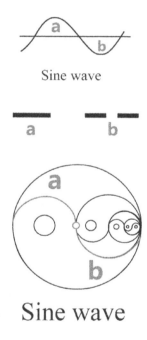

Sine wave

Sine wave

Figure 3 Holographic interference fringes and information unit

When we study energy waves, we usually pay attention to the amplitude, namely, its intensity, as well as its frequency, wavelength, and color, etc. By so doing, we overlook a very important concept--the dimensions of the sine wave or energy wave. When the concept of space mentioned before is included in the study, we could easily think of the dimensions of energy waves, that is, the degrees of flexibility of the energy waves. One-dimensional energy is line-based; two-dimensional energy is plane-based, while three-dimensional energy is cube based. When it comes to the fourth dimension, it transcends time and space. Therefore, the dimension of the energy wave is more important than its intensity. Under usual circumstances, most people ignore the concept of space, yet focus their attention on the frequency and its intensity. This is why when the modern New Age Movement tried to describe the relationship between mind and energy, they often used the concept of frequency, because frequency is described based on the understanding of waves in three-dimensional space.

Frequency is actually a function of time. It is the number of vibrations in unit time. The concept of frequency restricts us, however, because its relationship with time was confined to the concept of time as a constant factor. This is why it cannot really describe the energy relationship in the higher realms. So, what is the energy relationship in the higher realm? In other words, what is the relationship across different dimensions? I found that it was actually a projection relationship.

It was very simple. One dimension is the projection of two dimensions. Two dimensions is the projection of three dimensions. Three dimensions is the projection of four dimensions, and N-1 dimensions is the projection of N dimensions (N approaches infinity). Once we understand this projection relationship, we would have a complete understanding of the existence of the entire universe.

Why? Because we have discovered this vertical logical relationship, and this relationship can be connected totally with all the wisdom systems of human beings. According to an energy waves' transmission characteristics, another important concept is that any energy wave can be spread throughout the universe. It is a stone thrown into a pond, and the ripples extend throughout the entire pond. To put it simply, any energy wave would reach the whole universe and we know that everything is an energy wave.

Let's consider the reverse action. Take a single mass point in the universe as an example. Any energy wave that ripples across the entire universe would go past this point. The information contained in the energy wave--for example, frequency, amplitude, etc.--would affect this point. From this, we come to this simple concept: any mass point in the universe contains all information in the universe, and the relationship among all points. This is called the Law of Cosmic Holography. This, somehow, reflects a very important saying uttered by Buddha Sakyamuni when he reached enlightenment: "All sentient beings have the Tathagata's wisdom and virtue." It also reflects the Daoist principle that, "Dao is at any place and at any time," even to the effect that "Dao is in the urine and the shit." One single mass point contains the universal wisdom in N dimensions of space. When we have such understanding, we would understand that the descriptions of space and energy, the zero dimension or the N dimension (N approaches infinity), are the same thing. They all contact the entirety of information and the relationship among them. The evolution of all things in the universe happens among the zero dimension or the N dimension (N approaches infinity) space. Even though they might be the two extremes of dimensions, they are one entity.

The Chinese character "太", great, grand, extreme, is a very good and simple description of the universality of all information. To write the word "太", we only need to write the word "大", big, and then put a dot at the lower inner part. Hence, we have this word "太", a dot within the great space.

With the above explained, I have presented the core messages in my lectures. The language and the names, terms, and logical relationships used, are nothing I have created. They have been in the public domain for the past couple of hundred years. I have only extended the usage, and linked them up, and found the simple commonality and law among them. The system I use now can relate to, and be verified by, all other wisdom systems in human society. In the past thirty years, I have been using this wisdom system to communicate with practitioners and teachers of other religions and spiritual systems and have found it very convenient. I don't have to worry about the differences in context, and I can easily find the link among all wisdom systems while preserving the unique excellent features of each of them. I realize that higher realms in the universe are one entity.

In Buddhism, a Buddha is a person who has achieved unsurpassed, right enlightenment. Only the N Dimension (N approaches infinity) can be called unsurpassed. Only when the wisdom covers the N Dimension (N approaches infinity), can knowledge be called unsurpassed.

In Daoism, the ultimate highest realm is Wu Ji, no extreme. Only when it covers the knowledge in the N Dimension (N approaches infinity) can it be called unsurpassed. In Theology, God is the name for it, as it is unique, and only the Nth Dimension (N approaches infinity) can be called unique. When it comes to N-1 dimension, there are infinite numbers. And since the Nth Dimension is also the projection of all things, it is the ultimate dominant figure of all things. These would all fit the definition of a god. In the lectures that follow I will show you all the logical links in different categories, and I will show you the applications of all these in our daily lives.

Lecture 2 Multiple Wisdom Systems

From Difference to No Difference

Based on this core theoretical system, I want to discuss the comprehensive description of multiple systems. This description is by no means the whole truth, but it is equal to all it describes. It has a characteristic, namely the context it adopts. The scientific context is by far the most popular context in the world. It links with and verifies all wisdom systems and religions–for example, Buddhism, Daoism, Confucianism, Christianity, Muslim, and other religions, as well as all other spiritual systems. Since this context could link with all these systems, it becomes the connection for them all, and its essence enables us to understand the commonality of their multiple cultures.

A well-known Chinese saying goes like this: "To Seek Commonality and Reserve Differences." This saying is based on considerations in the three-dimensional world. We know that a three-dimensional world is one among the infinite number of worlds from zero to the Nth dimensions (N approaches infinity). When different people describe the same thing, differing definitions of the relevant names and terms create great differences.

Let me give you a simple example. When describing the same object in two different languages, very different semantic and phonetic forms might come into play. Those who do not grasp both these languages could not understand them and could not achieve proper communication. For example, the word "cup" in the Chinese language is "杯子". Two persons who do not simultaneously understand the forms in both the English and the Chinese language could not communicate with each other on this topic. Without a common language, a Buddhist finds it very difficult to debate a Christian. Two persons, only one of whom could only speak English, and the other could only speak Mandarin, would not understand each other. All because they have their own language system.

There are ample examples of our natural, cultural systems. Let's talk about culture. How should I interpret the word "culture"? In the Chinese language, we use two words - "wen" (文) and "hua" (化). Wen is the text, the information, while hua is the presence or manifestation. Hence, culture is a manifestation of information in the real world. Therefore, the information in different systems makes different cultures, which leads to the diversity of cultures. As human beings, we are often prone to interpret everything--and the cultures, links, and connections among them--from a single-culture perspective. In ancient times, when cultures were gradually taking form, each culture maintained its unique characteristics because of the restriction in time and space. When the unique character took form in each culture in the form of knowledge, it would maintain its description of the universe or a wisdom system, accumulated and passed down through generations. Such a description formed a unique cultural system. The uniqueness and inclusiveness of one cultural system are relatively independent of all other cultural systems.

With the development of human civilization, we have established more communication methods and have expanded many spaces for life. Many cultural intersections, integrations, and clashes have been witnessed. However, there is no complete integration of two cultural systems, and such integration would be difficult to realize. This is because we often view our world from a three-dimensional perspective. We always want to conquer the world using one culture. The underlying message is that each person trying to dominate the world thinks its culture is the best and is the best description of the truth. All religious civilizations on Earth are continually trying to expand their cultural territory.

Nowadays, the information a person could get access to in modern times is much more than it was in old times. We could get access to the information that accumulated in the entire history of human beings. The information, the people and the things that an ancient person had gone through in a lifetime could be experienced by modern people in a month. This is an era of multiculturalism for modern people.

The West's theology culture system appeared in ancient Egypt and the Middle East; Buddhism emerged in India, and Daoism and Confucianism arose in China. All these wisdom systems originated in the same age, the Axial Age.

These systems developed with their unique characteristics and continued to be passed down. With the development of human civilization, the clashes, communications and struggles among the cultures brought forth the major religions in our current world. During these processes, many smaller civilizations appeared and diminished.

Today, when we search for the truth, we'd be faced with several systems which are being used to describe the truth. Each of these systems is trying to tell one message: There is only one truth. If this is correct, why don't we select the core descriptions in all these systems regarding truth, and combine them? With the development of modern scientific civilization and information, we could easily search on the Internet and find information on all cultural systems in the world. It would be very challenging to summarize the differences and commonalities among all cultures. Even if for only two cultures, it would take one's entire life and effort to do so. Therefore, such exploration would be futile. In a three-dimensional world, the primary approach we could adopt is "To seek commonality and reserve differences." While we look for commonalities, we acknowledge the existence of those we disagree with.

According to the Projection Theory we discussed in the first chapter, the N-1th dimensional object is the projection on the Nth-dimensional space. We know this through the mechanical drawings of a three-dimensional object on a piece of paper (a two-dimensional media). We use the front view, side view, and top view of an item to project a three-dimensional object on a two-dimension media. This is an excellent example of the relationship between the projection source and the projection in the lower-dimension world. However, how many images could a three-dimension object have on a two-dimension space? Infinite!

I'd like to introduce here a concept in Einstein's Theory of Relativity. When an object moves fast, and when the speed approaches the speed of light, the length of this moving object will become shorter. This gives us an essential inspiration; when we observe an object in a three-dimensional world at different speeds, the object's shape will differ. Let us also keep in mind that speed is relative to time, as Speed = Distance ÷ Time.

Einstein's Theory of Relativity tells us another concept: when the speed of a moving object approaches the speed of light, time becomes slower. The word "becomes" is a very critical word. In a three-dimensional space, there are three important variants—the length, the width and the height—which are well known in the common knowledge system. However, in a three-dimensional space, there is also a constant element of time. And not merely time, but "objective time". In three-dimensional space, objective time, with objective seconds and objective minutes, is measured and determined by the frequency of oscillation of quartz at the Royal Greenwich Observatory.

But according to the Theory of Relativity, when the speed of a moving object approaches the speed of light, time slows down. This means time becomes a variant. Please note that, in a three-dimensional world where the speed varies, we could regard distance as the variant element, or we could regard time as the variant element. There are possibilities of these two variants existing in a three-dimension world: the size of an object, the amount of space it occupies, will be different if the time is a variant element. Such differences could be well described in the projection system.

This is interesting logic. I have mentioned before that the Nth dimension is the projection source of the N-1th dimension, and, in the lower dimensions, there is an infinite number of projections from a relatively higher dimension. I have given an example previously about the three-dimensional object being projected on a two-dimensional media, with all information concerning the three-dimensional object equally presented in the two-dimensional media. Further, I want to say that the fourth dimension is the projection source of the third dimension. For the fourth dimension, I say the rule becomes "To seek commonality and respect difference." I respect all reasonable existences of space because all projections come from the source.

What is the relationship between the projected images? When we look at them with the projection source, we could find the essence of their relationship. If we want to look for their commonalities in the projected images, it would not be meaningful and would waste our time and effort, as they are so different. We could only focus our attention on the individual images and the relationship between these images. It is crucial to look for commonalities in the higher dimensional space, while respecting the differences in the projected images. Only when we look at the projection source would we be able to truly see the logical relationship between the projected images.

A holographic view of the universe

1.1 The Space of Universe (Space)	**1.1.1 Multi-dimensional Space**	Zero Dimension— N Dimension (N= approaching infinity)
	1.1.2 Space and Time Relationship	The fourth dimension is time
		Time slows down when an object is moving at a velocity close to light
	1.1.3 The Relationships of Multi-dimensional Space	The relationships across dimensions is projection.
		Higher dimensions are projection sources.
1.2 Energy and Existence	**1.2.1 Quantum Attribution and Energy Waves**	Elementary particles have duality of wave-particle
		All existence are energy waves
		Nature of particles is the coherent imaging of energy waves.
	1.2.2 Freedom Level of Energy	The most important quality of energy waves is their level of freedom
	1.2.3 Multi-dimensional Energy	Lower-dimensional energy relationships is a projection of higher-dimensional energy relationships
		The zero dimension abounds in all the information of the universal space and mutual relationships
1.3 The Relationship Between Space And Energy	**1.3.1 Sine Wave (Simple Harmonic Wave)**	All complex waves are produced by the overlaying of simple harmonic waves according to Fourier transformation
	1.3.2 Interference of Energy waves	Two energy waves will produce interferences under certain conditions (create the five elements)
	1.3.3 Energy Wave Reoccurrence and Overlapping	The third energy wave renders energy at its same level of frequency, demonstrating a hologram, i.e. the three begets all things.

Figure 4 Generalized Holistic Universe Theory

I'd like to call the linking of the projected image to the projection source, "yuan" (缘), a word commonly used in Buddhism for affinity, connection, predestined relationship, etc.

What is "yuan" (缘)? The Chinese often say, "There is (strong) yuan (缘) between us." "Follow the yuan" (缘). What exactly is yuan (缘), then?

Using the description of the projected image and the projection source makes it easier for us to understand yuan (缘). Yuan (缘) is the relationship established in the projection source. We have encounters with many, many people in our lifetime. We may have a close relationship with some, while limited encounters with others. These relationships have been established or determined in the higher-dimensional space. The reason for us to meet today is because the conditions established in the higher-dimensional space have matured in our current dimension.

Now, it will be easier for us to understand why, in Buddhism, the beginning or the origin, and the ending, are not discussed. The Buddha expounded only on conditional origination, as all comes from the projection source. In the fourth-dimensional space, time is a variant element. The beginning and end in a three-dimensional world have been transcended in a four-dimensional space. When time is a variant element, there is no beginning and there is no end; there is no past, present, or future. The measuring of the beginning and the end in a three-dimensional world is meaningless in a four-dimensional space.

The commonalities in the projection source are the more essential messages. This is why I use the term "To seek commonality and respect difference" to describe it. In Daoism, this is called "Earth follows Heaven." （地法天）
The Earth is three dimensional, and Heaven is four dimensional, which is a higher dimension. When I seek commonality and respect differences, I enter the realm of "Earth follows Heaven", because the three-dimensional Earth is showing the images projected from the four-dimensional Heaven.

From the fourth dimension up to the Nth dimension (N approaches infinity), there is a gradual increment of states whereby the states come "to Summarize Commonality and Understand Difference". For example, from the fifth dimensional perspective, all information appearing in the fourth dimensional space can be seen as clear as day. The same rule applies when comparing the sixth dimensional space and the fifth dimensional space. Therefore, from the fourth dimensions up, the higher dimensions "summarize commonality and understand difference".

When I say, "to summarize commonality and understand difference," I refer to the realm of "Heaven follows the Dao." Upward from the third-dimensional space, there are endless spaces, all the way to the Nth dimensional space. The levels become higher and higher. In Daoism, this is called "Heaven follows Dao" (天法道).

When in the Nth dimension (N approaches infinity), all things are integrated into one. In this realm, there is no difference. That's why I describe it as "No commonality and no difference." When N approaches infinity, it enters the original state of the projection source. In Daoism, this is called "Dao follows nature" (道法自然). This is the highest state level. It also matches the description of the status of a Buddha, who has achieved the complete, unsurpassed, and perfect Enlightenment. In Daoism, it is also called "wu ji" (无极), which exists at any place and any time. In western theology, it is the unique presence, the integration of all things in one. It is also the omnipresent and the omnipotent. It is the projection source of all things. Because of all these, I say, multiple cultural systems, or wisdom systems, become integrated as one at the Nth-dimensional space (N approaches infinity).

Of course, we human beings could use many descriptions to describe different energy levels. However, when all wisdom systems are at their ultimate level, they would be free of any form, and they would all be beyond description by any form. When I truly understand this, I would truly understand Buddha Sakyamuni's words in the Diamond Sutra, "If anyone says the Tathagata is expounding the Dharma, he would be slandering the Buddha", and also that "He who sees me by outward appearance and seeks me in sound, treads the heterodox path and will not see the Tathagata." In the Christian teachings, the description that God is the only uniqueness is for the purpose of avoiding attachment to any level of energy presence. In other words, no worship of idols is allowed. In Islam, Allah is also described as a formless existence.

In the Nth-dimensional space, this is a concept of relativity. In this concept, it is a never-ending state. Just like the saying in Daoism, "The Dao which can be described is not the universal and eternal Dao." We use language or logic to describe the truth, yet the language, or the logic itself is not truth. Through the description, I see the commonality of all systems, religious or otherwise. The commonality between our world and the ultimate wisdom realm is the same, and they could verify each other. The essence of commonality is the same, no matter where it exists. A cake could be cut in millions of ways, vertically or horizontally, but the essence of the cake is the same. With this understanding, and also the knowledge of the ways of cutting a cake, i.e., the methods of analysis, I would respect each and every way of cutting the cake, i.e., the interpretation.

The content of this lecture is a broad summary. I'll elaborate the contents in future lectures. Each wisdom system is profound. Our scientific context helps us in our exploration of the commonality and difference among those systems.

Lecture 3 The Wisdom of Buddhism

A Detailed Explanation on the Relationship of the Cosmic Energies

From a holistic perspective, Buddhism is a wisdom system that has the most complete, detailed, and accurate description of the universe, ranging from the zero dimension to the Nth dimension (N approaches infinity). Buddha Sakyamuni expounded his teachings for over forty years, and he inspired beings at various levels. He provided a detailed description of the beings at multiple levels.

Let us first have a look at the definition of "Buddha." In Buddhism, the Buddha is equivalent to complete, unsurpassed, and perfect Enlightenment. This description matches exactly the cosmic wisdom of the Nth dimension (N approaches infinity). It is the Nth dimension (N approaches infinity), which could be regarded as "unsurpassed." The complete, unsurpassed, and perfect enlightenment is a complete description of the entire cosmic wisdom. When the Surangama Sutra discusses the Tathagatagarbha, the Tathagata Store, it is actually

31

discussing space. According to the sutra, there are three levels of Tathagatagarbha. The first level is called the Void Tathagatagarbha; the second level is called Non-Void Tathagatagarbha, and the third level is called Non-Non-Void Tathagatagarbha. How should one try to understand these three concepts in their various spaces?

The Void Tathagatagarbha refers to the Nth dimension (N approaches infinity). Being in this dimension, it has no appearance of any form. When N approaches infinity, it will surpass all intermediate levels. The word "non", meaning "void" or "emptiness", actually includes all presence without omission. In Buddhism, the concept of "voidness" does not mean "nothing". Actually, it includes everything, but it does not dwell on a single form. The Non-Void Tathagatagarbha refers to the zero dimension. It represents the "current" moment. At this current moment, at one certain point in time and space, a Mass Point which does not occupy any space contains the information which has the connections among all information in all wisdom systems. This is called Non-Void Tathagatagarbha. This is the law of cosmic holography, and the Mass Point is called the holographic point, which contains all existence. The Non-Non-Void Tathagatagarbha includes all dimensions from the fourth dimension to the N-1th dimension. It contains all levels of existence. When the third dimension is voided, it enters the fourth dimension, and the progress continues upwards. In each of the dimensions, each Mass Point, at a certain moment, can reach the Nth dimension, and also the zero dimension. This is why I say that

Buddhism is a wisdom system which has the most complete, detailed and precise descriptions of the universe.

In Buddhism, there are two more important concepts which describe the entire space. The first one is "wu lou" (无漏), which means "no leakage." The complete full coverage in a coordinate system, from zero dimension to the Nth dimension, is called "no leakage." It means that no message is left outside this system. It also contains the relationship among all information. The other concept is called "infinite" or "measureless". It is also a description of the Nth dimension (N approaches infinity). There is another infinity which is at the zero dimension. This Mass Point contains measureless information, and the link among all this information. These two are the main characteristics of the term "infinite" as described in Buddhism.

I have previously mentioned that the single-dimensional space is a line. The two-dimensional space is a plane, a surface, while the three-dimensional space is a cube. There are different amounts of information in different dimensional spaces, and the information embraces each other. But why is it that we human beings can only see the three-dimensional world, and we cannot see the world beyond the fourth dimension?

The fourth dimensional space is the projection source of the three-dimensional world. If we want to see the projection source, namely, beyond the fourth dimension, we would have to seek inwardly. Through the concept of a projection source, we already know that there are an infinite number of dots in a single-dimensional world, an infinite number of lines in a two-dimensional world, and an infinite number of planes in a three-dimensional world.

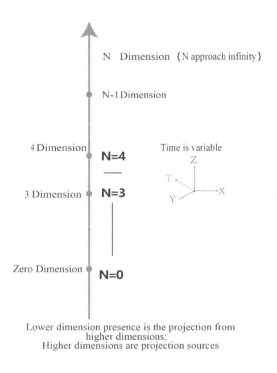

Figure 5 Multi-dimensional space concept

We also know that, with any increase of one dimension, there would be an infinite increase in the amount of information. It is like that in Buddhism, where there are many different levels of heavens–for example the heavens of Mahabrahmana, Trayastrimsa, Tsuti, Nirmaarati, Parinirmita-vasavartin, etc. The difference between dimensions is like the difference between human and ant. That's why, through the concept of relative space, we are able to learn the highest realm levels of the Buddha, which is the difference between the wisdom of the Nth dimension

(N approaches infinity) and the knowledge of our three-dimensional space. Our three-dimensional knowledge, compared with the Nth dimensional wisdom, is basically nothing.

Why? Because $\frac{3}{\infty} = 0$; $\frac{4}{\infty} = 0$ and $\frac{5}{\infty} = 0$. From this, a simple conclusion is that any number compared with infinity equals zero. Although this is a mathematical concept, it matches the concept stated in the Diamond Sutra: "All things contrived are like a dream, an illusion, a bubble, a shadow, a dewdrop or lightning. One should have such a view."

If, when looking inward, we purify our minds, we can surpass obstacles and achieve the inner wisdom that is approaching infinity. Then this formula becomes $\frac{\infty}{\infty} = 1$. This is the state of "Heaven and man integrated as one" (天人合一): a state of presence everywhere in all realms. Therefore, now, it is not difficult to understand the meaning of "Heaven and man integrated as one". The level of comprehension of this concept "Heaven and man integrated as one" exceeds one's level of understanding. Some would say, this concept explains the relationship between us and the limited universe which is visible to us. This is far from the reality. Why? Because what we can see now does not exceed the three-dimensional world. But the relationship between us and a three-dimensional world is limited. The concept of "Heaven and man integrated as one" (天人合一) states the relationship of existence between us and the fourth, fifth, up to the Nth dimensional space (N approaches infinity).

The holographic view of the universe based on the concept of "Heaven and man integrated as one" is a holistic view of integrated cosmic information. Such holistic view enables us to see the universe as a grand picture, and see all the links and connections among all information in the universe. This, then, could be referred to as "Heaven and Man Integrated as One". When I try to understand "wu lou" (no-leakage), "infinite," and "Heaven and Man Integrated as One," using the concept of space, I am able to understand the great comprehensiveness of Buddhism.

Now, let's discuss a fundamental concept in Buddhism, Dependent Origination. Some call it the Conditioned Genesis. As I explained before, matters in the lower dimensional world are the projected images of matters in the higher dimensional world. The relationship between them I have called "yuan" (缘). The English rendering of yuan is "condition," "connection," or "affinity". All things that could be seen in our world are somehow connected with their projection source. The relationship among all people falls into the definition of yuan. When the projection sources of relationships haven't eventualized in our three-dimensional world, I'd call it the "immature affinity". When the conditions are ripe, namely, when they meet on a point of time and space, I'd call it "affinity eventualized".

The word "yuan" has been subtly and delicately used in Buddhism. Why? It has transcended our three-dimensional perceptions. It is hard to understand the difference between yuan and relationship. When we look vertically at the spatial difference, we would understand the relationship is between a projection source and its projected image. Why is the term "yuan" used in Buddhism? In the three-dimensional world, time is a constant element, with a beginning and an end. In the four-dimensional space, time is a variant element, hence, nothing has a beginning or end. In Buddhism, as mentioned before, there is a term, "Dependent Origination." Existence depends on the yuan. The Yuan is the connection between the projection source and the presence in the lower dimension. When I use this logic to explain "Dependent Origination," I understand the rigor in the Buddhism wisdom.

However, as human beings who live in this three-dimensional world, we always like to expect a beginning and end in descriptions of the universe. So-called science is strongly upheld by people in the three-dimensional world as the truth. The biggest conceptual obstacle in our three-dimensional world is our perception of time–namely, we take time as a constant element. Such view hinders our exploration of the micro world, as time cannot be split into small enough elements. In the smallest possible time frame, we could not precisely capture the spatial position of any micro matter. This is why we call the formation of electrons an electron cloud, which is subject to the Uncertainty Principle according to Quantum Physics. The Uncertainty Principle, first introduced in 1927 by the German physicist Werner Heisenberg, states that the more precisely the position of a particle is determined, the less precisely its momentum can be predicted from its initial conditions, and vice versa.

The obstacle preventing us from comprehending the macro-world is the limitedness of time. Things that are one hundred light-years away are not our concern. However, when time becomes a variant element, or the dimension is being raised, we could turn one second into 1000 years, 1 million years, or 10 billion years. Matters happening in the micro-world could then be explored clearly. We could also shrink 10 thousand years into one minute and capture and pull the micro-worlds outer space right in front of us. This is called the Folding of Space.

Imagine there is a piece of thread, and the tip of one end is Point A, and the other end is Point B. For an ant to travel from Point A to Point B on a stretched flat line, would take a certain period of time. If the thread is folded in the middle, and Point A and Point B become overlapped, an ant could reach from Point A to Point B in no time. This is the so-called Folding of Space. The folding of space could only happen in a higher dimensional space. In some literary fiction, teleportation is often described. They see it as travelling through a space tunnel, or wormhole, which is merely terminology to explain the situation of space movement, or when time becomes a variant element in the fourth or higher-dimensional space.

What is "Dependent origination, and voidness is its nature" in Buddhism? Nature is original nature, or essence. The form of an object in a three-dimensional world is related to the energy in the four-dimensional space. This rule applies to the relationship between a lower dimension and its immediate higher dimension. In other words, the nature of the energy in the higher dimension determines its presence in the immediate lower dimension. Ultimately, the nature of the energy in the Nth dimension (N approaches infinity) determines the form in the N-1th dimension. When one achieves voidness in the three-dimensional world, they can enter the fourth-dimensional space. This rule applies all the way up to the N-1th dimension. When Nth dimension is achieved (N approaches infinity), the nature of the dimension is the nature of voidness. It doesn't mean, in this state, that there is nothing. On the contrary, it means that there is everything, and all things exist in it. This description, namely the Buddhists' description, reflects the energy relationship between all various levels, and at the same time, it reflects the highest wisdom by using the term, "Dependent Origination, and Voidness is its Nature". The Nth dimension (N approaches infinity) is the projection source of all things, and the presence of the Nth dimension is the very origin of dependent origin–the realm of truth, but only one truth. Because, in the N-1th dimension, there can be an infinite number of projections. Therefore, what we see, what we think, and feel, all fall into the energy relationship, and they are all false images. The true image has no form. But even though it does not appear in any form, it contains all the basic conditions of all forms.

There is another important concept called the Law of Causality (因果律). The usual explanation provided for the Law of Causality in the past is somewhat not very convincing. I'd like to use a simple way to explain, namely, the Law of Action and Reaction in physics. When I knock on the table, the harder I knock, the more pain my hand will feel. This is the Law of Action and Reaction in the three-dimensional world. However, in the four-dimensional world, time is a variant element. Even though an action's force still brings a response of the same strength and opposite direction, the reaction time may not be simultaneous.

Opportunities exist in the lives of all people. If a person who is in the process of developing his career is provided with an important opportunity, but he is in a bad mood, and he didn't take on the opportunity, or he didn't have the capability to take advantage of the opportunity, he would miss it. Even if he could identify it, due to his bad mood, he might only be able to use only 20-30% of his potential. Or, he might not be able to identify the opportunity. On the contrary, if a person is happy and cheerful and positive, he may easily identify the opportunity, and take it on. Furthermore, he may act better than his usual performance. This example tells us the importance of having a good mood, especially at critical moments for success.

We know it is difficult for one to keep having a good mood all the time. It is a task for self-cultivation. One could use psychological measures to achieve mental balance and maintain a positive attitude. Life experience would also help one to achieve mental balance. For those setbacks or failures that we have not yet encountered, how could we still maintain a positive attitude? Mental power, specifically the mental strength that comes from understanding the Law of Causality. Accessing the Law of Causality is a fast way to navigate out of any negative situation or setback. Why is this? Usually, when people face disastrous situations and do not have a correct understanding of the Law of Causality, they will keep complaining. They complain that they are so unfortunate. On the contrary, those who have a good understanding of the Law of Causality would reflect on the possible causes in the past. They would be of the view that the current misfortune results from karmic debt from the past. Imagine how you would feel after you've paid off a long-due debt. You could come out of the setback swiftly. You would not feel sad. You would, on the contrary, feel very relieved.

Through an understanding of the Law of Causality, the wisdom in Buddhism, one could achieve a quick turn-around in a negative situation and could maintain a positive state. The Law of Causality is not a passive action. On the contrary, it is a reminder in each moment of life to reflect, to adjust and to change one's wrong attitude.

Another concept full of wisdom in Buddhism is the description of the existence of space and time in our universe. The term used is the "illusionary amalgamation of the four great elements" (四大假合). All forms of matter in the three-dimensional world, our body included are illusionary amalgamations of the four great elements, namely, earth, water, fire, and wind. These four elements in this perspective are not what are suggested by the names in our common understanding. They represent the level of freedom of energy. The earth element has, for example, the lowest level of freedom. I describe it as a relatively stable status of energy interference and imaging. Water, being in the form of liquid, flows, and has more freedom when compared with solid earth. Fire is in the state of burning. It is visible, and can be felt, and it has more freedom than water. Wind represents the air, the turbulence, and has more freedom than fire. There is a gradual increase in the level of freedom in these four great elements, and they have been described as the four basic elements in the world of form.

In Hinduism, they use five elements–namely, earth, water, fire, and wind, and space (or emptiness)–to describe the universe. The description of space matches the Ether named by Aristotle. In Buddhism, the aforementioned four great elements form matter in space. To explore further, space is actually the voidness, an energy status for entering a higher-dimensional world. In Daoism, Qi (or Chi) is used to describe the energy. In its traditional Chinese form, Qi is "氣", with the word "rice" underneath. At the interface between the third and the fourth dimensions, the character for Qi is "气+火", but with the word "fire" underneath. This interface state is the Quantum State in modern science. Going further up, we encounter another Qi, written in the form "炁", which reflects the Genuine Qi, the high-dimensional energy. What is the Genuine Qi? It is the projection source, and the essence of things is closely related to our body, and to the entire energy field in the universe. I will elaborate on this in the next lecture.

When talking about the relationship of Buddhism and science, there is another very important topic we must cover here in this lecture - the concept of form and emptiness. Previously I mentioned that the fundamental existence in the universe is the Sine Wave, which is an energy wave. When two Sine waves meet, and when they have the same amplitude and frequency, interference will occur at a specific location in space. The result is that there would be increased oscillations in some places, and in other places, the energies will be offset and will create an alternative dark and bright interference fringe. These interference stripes created by the two energies will create the "form." When there is no interference, no forms will be created, and this stage is called "emptiness." In the Heart Sutra, we read that "Form is emptiness, emptiness is form; emptiness is no other than form, form too is no other than emptiness."

Further, "they are not defiled, they are not undefiled; they are not deficient, and they are not complete." No more will be created if a form has been created, and no less will be deleted if no form has been created. The Heart Sutra continues to say, "Likewise, feelings, perceptions, mental formations, and consciousness are all empty." Each of the feelings, perceptions, mental formations, and consciousness shows a function of the energy, yet these types are not in existence in any form, and each is related to the concept of energy. We also read from the Diamond Sutra, one should "give rise to the mind without dwelling on anything." The mind here means a deeper consciousness.

When compared with deep consciousness, surface consciousness is an obstacle. For example, when I raise a piece of paper in front of my eyes, a two-dimensional object, it will block the link between me and the three-dimensional world. When I remove this piece of paper, I will see the items in the three-dimensional world, in which there is boundless information. Likewise, only when I eliminate attachment and consciousness in the three-dimensional world can I achieve four-dimensional wisdom. The essence of all spiritual cultivation is to "eliminate wandering thoughts" to let go and become "empty". When letting go of the three-dimensional world and becoming empty in it, a "genuine emptiness" of the three-dimensional world is formed, and it will create the information, named "Miao you" (妙有), the subtle existence, in the fourth-dimensional space. When combined, it is called the "subtle existence in the genuine emptiness." The same applies to the higher dimensions' progress until the Nth dimension (N approaches infinity). The alternative presence of the genuine emptiness and the subtle existence is spontaneous. When we do not attach to any single dimension, we can enter the higher dimensions' inner realm. The detachment is called "without dwelling on anything." The mind here is the true mind, the true essence of one's nature.

There are many high-dimensional practices and cultivations in Buddhism, such as the scriptures' text and the mantras. There will be the energy associated with the text in our secular world wherever there is a text. The reason is that each form is a presence of the projected image of energy in our three-dimensional world from the projection source. The same applies to the text of Buddhist scriptures--for example, the Diamond Sutra and the text just quoted. When I read the scripture, which is a projection of the Nth dimensional world (N approaches infinity), I resonate and oscillate with the high-level energy. This is a high-dimensional practice and cultivation. Buddhist mantras have the same power. Mantras are sound energy from the high-dimensional world. When I chant a mantra, my consciousness resonates and oscillates with the high-level energy. There are various mantras in different dimensional worlds, and the nature of the energy is different. Such mantras would have different power in our three-dimensional world to resolve the clustered and entangled energies. Both Buddhist scriptures and mantras have very high-level energy.

I'd like to give you another example. We are all familiar with the mantra "Amitabha" in the practice of the Pure Land School of Buddhism. When this word "Amitabha" is translated, it means, "infinite light and infinite life". To adopt this saying in the scientific context, I would say, the infinite light is the cosmic energy from the Nth dimensional universe (N approaches infinity); while the infinite life is the biggest energy wave in the universe. When I chant the mantra "Amitabha", I am resonating my body with the energy. In doing so, I am consolidating the imperfect waves in and around me. This is like Power Line Communication technology through which I can put all kinds of energies and waves in a bundle, regardless of their nature. I think it resonates with what is called "reaching Pure Land with residue karma" in Pure Land Buddhism. The abundance and profundity of Buddhism, when read with scientific logic, can inspire in enormous ways. Each Buddhist scripture, i.e., the Heart Sutra, or the Diamond Sutra, or the Platform Sutra of the Sixth Patriarch, warrants independent research. With the introduction of scientific logic, we'd be able to explore and interpret more of these scriptures.

Lecture 4 The Wisdom of Daoism

Heaven and Man Integrated as One, and Dao Follows Nature

How does Daoism describe the different levels of the entire universe? In chapter thirty-eight of the Dao De Jing, we read that "When Dao is lost, there is virtue (De, 德) left; when De is lost, there is humanity (Ren, 仁); when humanity is lost, there is justice (Yi, 义); when justice is lost, there is etiquette (Li, 礼); when etiquette is lost, there is benefit (Li, 利)." What does all this mean? Dao represents the wisdom of the Nth dimensional space (N approaches infinity). When it comes to the N-1th dimension, the Dao is lost. From N-1th dimension to the Fourth dimension, virtue is the prevailing characteristic of all these dimensions. In the Chinese language, we have used "great virtue" and "high expectations", and "heavy virtue carries all things" to describe virtue. When virtue is lost, one enters the third dimension, a dimension with the characteristics of humanity. The word for humanity, Ren, is formed with a person on the left and a figure "two" on the right. In my

47

opinion, this word Ren signifies two men. One is a man of a physical form, and the other is an invisible man of energy. Or, I shall say, one is a man in the form of particles, and the other is in the form of waves. Ren represents great love. As everyone knows, love is the greatest energy that can be felt in the three-dimensional world. Through the Dao De Jing, we have come to understand the descriptions of the different levels of the entire universe from a Daoist's perspective, which is highly compatible with the descriptions that I have given. In Daoism, "Heaven and Men Integrated as One" is one of the most important doctrines.

What does "Heaven and Man Integrated as One" mean? The world in which we live is a three-dimensional world. Compared with the Nth dimensional universe (N approaches infinity), our world is minimal, next to the presence of existence. When we understand that 3: Infinity = 0, so is 4, 5, or any actual figure, because, when compared with the infinite dimensional universe, the limited number of dimensions, medium in size, is next to nothing, and could be considered non-existing. This echoes the description in the Diamond Sutra that "All things contrived are like a dream, an illusion, a bubble, a shadow, a dewdrop or lightning. One should have such a view."

If, through cultivation, one was able to enter higher and higher dimensions, and one could get closer and closer to the Nth dimension, the number of the dimension he would be in would be close to infinity. Therefore, the formula becomes Infinity: Infinity = 1. This would be the situation where one is truly integrated with heaven. However, currently in our three-dimensional world, we are restricted in our mindset and are only able to deal with relationships in a limited sense. These relationships include the relationship between heaven and men, the universe and men, and spatial objects and men. However, from the Nth dimension one could see the universe from a perspective far beyond our imagination and knowledge. The genuine concept of "Heaven and Men Integrated as One" means that the wisdom level of one person is the same as that in the Nth dimension.

There is another very subtle dimension—the zero dimension. I have talked about it in the first lecture. The zero dimension is a Mass Point (without interior) which could not be further divided. According to the nature of the transmission of waves, each Mass Point in the universe contains the full information of the universe, and the connections among all information. In other words, it contains the full wisdom of the universe. In fact, the Nth dimension has the same nature as the Zero dimension. This is the description of the entire universe, and this description contains all the information in the universe. This could be called the genuine concept of "Heaven and Men Integrated as One". Through such a cosmic view, we would be able to have a comprehensive view of the universe, of the Dao, and understand why it is everywhere and at any time.

Let me try and illustrate this through a Chinese character. Once again, I'll use the word Tai, "太", as in "tai ji". As explained before, the character Da, "大" represents the Nth dimension (N approaches infinity) and the dot underneath it represents the zero dimension, a Mass Point. Therefore, this character Tai represents the entire universe. And, this is the greatness and subtlety of the Chinese language.

Let us now have a look at the distribution of energy in the different dimension levels. To explain the distribution-- from simple Energy Stacking to the complex formation of real-world objects-- I would need to first explain the numerology of the Yi Jing (I Ching).

We are talking about a single Sine wave. When there is another wave of the same frequency and amplitude, under certain conditions, these two waves would start to interfere with each other. Due to the characteristics of energy distribution in space, part of the waves will be strengthened while part will diminish, which will result in the interference fringes. These fringes are reflected by the term "se" (色) or form, in Buddhism. When the conditions for interference are not matured, despite the existence of the energies, there would not be forms. This condition is described in Buddhism as "kong" (空), or "empty" or "void". Hence the famous saying in the Heart Sutra, "Form is emptiness, emptiness is form; emptiness is not other than form, form too is not other than emptiness." Further, "they are not defiled, they are not undefiled; they are not deficient, and they are not complete".

The stacking and interference of two waves could be described in a formula:

$$(a + b)^2 = 1$$

When this formula is extended, it becomes: $a^2 + b^2 + ab + ba = 1$, and they correspond to the "Tai Yang", the fire element; "Tai Yin", the water element; "Shao Yang", the wood element; and "Shao Yin", the metal element, as have been described in the Yi Jing. The combined energy of all these reflects the earth element. The energies of the Five Elements are actually the result of the interference of two waves, manifesting in the distribution of the five energies.

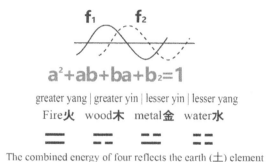

$$a^2+ab+ba+b_2=1$$

greater yang | greater yin | lesser yin | lesser yang

Fire火 wood木 metal金 water水

The combined energy of four reflects the earth (土) element

Each holographic interference fringes
is a reflection of one information unit.

Figure 6 Holographic interference fringes and the distribution of the five energies

As mentioned before, the interference fringes, or stripes, are called "images". If we put on the wall a picture of the holographic interference fringes, we would know, based on the principles of optics, that this picture consisted of an infinite number of interference fringes, as each of the fringes is a reflection of one information unit.

When we look at the interference fringe from a different perspective–from the left, or from the right–we would see a different picture. This demonstrates that the energy wave of the mind is different in different people.

The energy wave of the mind in this picture is different from the reconstructed wave. Hence, a third energy wave appears, namely: $(a + b)^3 = 1$.

When this formula is extended, it becomes:

$$a^3 + aab + aba + baa + abb + bab + bba + b^3 = 1$$

The extended formula above corresponds with the Eight Trigrams, the Ba Gua. Let me put it this way: the Eight Trigrams represent the images of the most basic object forms in our three-dimensional world. These three lines, solid or broken, are the three interference stripes. When the images of the eight trigrams, or, of the eight pieces of information, being the compilation of yet unrevealed information, are stacked together, they form the sixty-four formations, which represent the basic element of the entire existence of objects in our three-dimensional world. I call them the "basic spectrums". This, as mentioned before, is the numerology of the Yi Jing.

$$(a+b)^3 = 1$$

$$a^3 + baa + aba + bba + aab + bab + abb + b^3 = 3$$

乾	兑	离	震	巽	坎	艮	坤
☰	☱	☲	☳	☴	☵	☶	☷
qian	diu	li	zhen	xun	kan	gen	kun

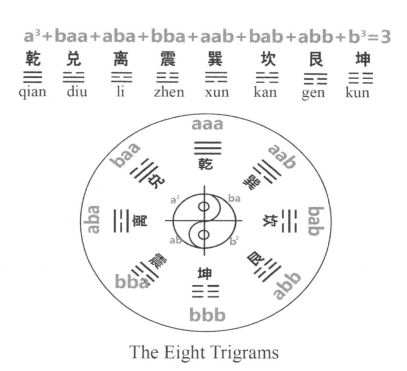

The Eight Trigrams

Figure 7 Numerology of the Yi Jing

If we could explain this numerology to those who do not understand the Chinese language or the abstract text in the Yi Jing, they would be able to understand that Yi Jing describes the origin of things in this universe. The energies of the single wave, the two waves, and the three waves,

53

correspond with the concept of "Dao produces One, One produces Two, Two produces Three, and Three produces all things." In this three-dimensional world, all things could be put into one of the sixty-four categories, which are the basic forms of distribution. When, furthermore, these sixty-four forms of distribution are stacked together, they represent all things in our universe. The Yi Jing describes the law of such stacking. With the change of time and space, the images of all things change, too.

From the above discussions we would understand that the third energy wave is the most important one to us, as what we are able to see is determined by the images rendered by our third energy wave. And, the third energy wave is actually emanated by the observer. The energy spectrum, namely the frequency characteristics, is a manifestation of the observer's knowledge. This is described in Buddhism as "Karma". What we see in this world is a projection of what we know. Based on what we know, our mind creates a world. This is why the Buddhists say, "All Dharma is subject to the mind" and "all forms are created by the mind."

However, the entire universe is not a three-dimensional world. Let's have a look at this picture of Tai Ji. This picture could be drawn with one continuous line.

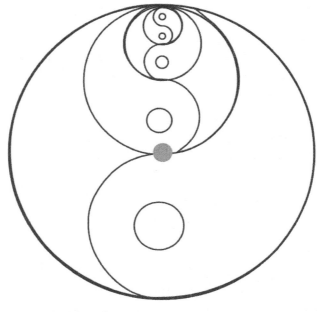

Multi-dimensional
Tai Ji diagram

Figure 8 Multi-dimensional Tai Ji diagram

We could continue to make it smaller, and smaller, until infinity; we could also continue to make it larger, and larger, until infinity. I call this picture the Multi-dimensional Tai Ji. It demonstrates the fact that in different dimensions in the universe, there exist the energy distributions in the forms such as Liang Yi (Two Spheres), Si Xiang (Four Forms), and Ba Gua (Eight Trigrams). In other words, there exist different life forms in different dimensions. The energy relationship that we could feel in the three-dimensional world, even in the four-dimensional space, is also distributed in this same pattern. This is what I refer to as the horizontal and vertical cosmic views.

In the wisdom of Daoism, there is a system which is closely related to us. That is Chinese medicine, which has its origin in the Yi Jing, a system with folded or stacked energies. As mentioned before, all things in our world are images resulting from interference fringes of energy waves. The most important factor for images to be formed is the relative balance of energies. In other words, when two energy waves are in balance, their interference fringes result in images. The balance of energy, the balance of Yin and the Yang, is the foundation of all things in the universe.

In Chinese medicine, illness or disease has its location, or "nest" -- its situation, manifesting images. When one is ill, he is not in a state of balance in terms of energy. The treatment, therefore, in Chinese medicine, is to interrupt the imbalance, and resume the balance in the body. When this is achieved, one becomes healthy. Western medicine uses an adversarial method to combat illness or disease. For example, a counter-Sine wave would be used for treating a Sine wave condition. At a precise calculation, the illness could be offset. However, the counter-Sine wave could harm other parts of the body, and result in side effects. This is one of the characteristics of western medicine. When a doctor writes his prescriptions, he always needs to tell his patient that, in the hope of treating the targeted illness, this medication could bring harm to other parts of your body. Chinese medicine, on the other hand, treats illness by way of balancing energies in accordance with the Law of the

Five Elements in a systematic way. Energy balance is the goal of treatment in Chinese medicine.

One of the principles in Chinese medicine is the theory of Ziwu Liuzhu (子午流注). Ziwu Liuzhu is a method in traditional Chinese medicine which applies the best use of time when an acupoint's energy is at its ultimate level. The distribution of energy in any given dimension is in the forms of Liang Yi (Two Spheres), Si Xiang (Four Forms), and Ba Gua (Eight Trigrams). On the time axis in the fourth dimension, such distribution is in place as well. With this as a general rule, one would be able to see the patterns of changes, and one would understand that good Chinese medicine practitioners treat illness with different methods at different times and places. We know that, at different times of the day, our organs' ability to repair themselves depends on the strength of their inner energy. Each of our organs' characteristic energy distribution could be described corresponding to the five elements--namely metal, wood, water, fire and earth. When time is considered in this dynamic process, the theory of Ziwu Liuzhu comes into play. Therefore, if a good practitioner could determine the right time for the right energy to be at its peak, he would easily help the patient achieve energy balance among the organs. On the contrary, if a practitioner does not know this theory, or applied treatment at the wrong time, he might not receive good treatment results. What's worse, he could bring negative effects to his patient. This is why Chinese practitioners attach great importance to the time of treatment.

Figure 9 Ten Heavenly Stems (China Buddhism Encyclopedia)

Now, I'd like to mention another important theory–the "heavenly stems" and the "earthly branches". The sequential numbers of Jia, Yi and Bing all the way to Ren and Gui, are the ten "heavenly stems", while the Zi, Chou and Yin, all the way to Xu and Hai, are the twelve "earthly branches". The "heavenly stems" and the "earthly branches" system represents a vertical distribution of energy associated with time. It follows the energy relationship of the five elements. The earthly branches represent the energy relationship in our three-dimensional world, and represent the horizontal distribution of energy. The moment the heavenly stems and the earthly branches are stacked, the vertical and horizontal energies interfere with each other, and this is the moment when all things in the three-dimensional world are created. In other words, the moment the energies from a higher dimension are projected in the lower dimension is the moment of creation. For example, the birth time of a person, as described in "eight characters", is just such a critical moment that decides the energy in the three-dimensional world. This point of time contains the energy information, which could be interpreted to tell (or predict) all things that are to happen in that

person's life and all people that he is going to meet, too.

Figure 10 Twelve Earthly Branches (China Buddhism Encyclopedia)

Let me give you another example. My hand is a three-dimensional object. If I put my open palm in between a light source and the wall, a shadow–the shape of my palm–would appear on the wall. If one is on that two-dimensional wall, and tries to trace the outline of the palm, and started from where my thumb is, he wouldn't know what would be coming next. However, when viewed from the three-dimensional world, away from the wall, one could easily see the whole picture on the two-dimensional wall.

By the same theory, when viewing from a higher dimension, all things in the lower dimension would be very clear. This is the essence of the Heavenly Stems Theory. Provided with the correct birth time of a person, a good Chinese medicine practitioner would also be able to calculate and tell which organ would be in an inferior state, and when this patient would become ill.

Now let's have a look at the acupoints and the meridians in a body according to Chinese medicine. It is very hard to locate the acupoints by physical measurements, as they cannot be felt externally. What exactly is an acupoint? It is a focal point of energy from a higher dimension. For a camera to take a picture, it needs a lens which has a focal point to convert a three-dimensional object onto a two-dimensional film. The focal point is usually unknown to most people. Actually, the focal point is a point which enables the four-dimensional energy to be projected in our three-dimensional bodies, organs, and cells. A series of focal points of the same nature form a meridian. This is the inner connection between the Chinese medicine system and the higher dimensional energies.

The treatment in Chinese medicine, using acupoints and meridians, is likened to spectrum management in the principles of light. The energy level of the focal points located at different spots can be adjusted to accommodate different amounts of light going through the aperture. The larger the aperture, the more energy.

The adjusting of the aperture is the key, which achieves a balance of energy among the images. The balance of energy is the healthy state. From the above explanations we can understand the close relationship between Chinese medicine and high dimensional energy.

The Symphony of High Dimensional Wisdoms

In today's medical education system, western education methods are in a more dominant position, and a lot of the essence of Chinese medicine has been neglected. When we truly understand the spirit in the Yi Jing and the Yellow Emperor's Inner Classics, and understand the energy relationships within the body, we would understand the levels of Chinese medicine practitioners. There are three levels: the low, the medium and the high practitioners. It is because of the different approaches to medicine that there are these three different levels of Chinese medical practitioners.

The lower practitioners, in my description, are the ones who can only use the three-dimensional view to treat illness. Such practitioners could not even compete with those who are practicing western medicine, as they would not have their enriched experiences and problem-solving skills.

The medium level practitioners would apply the higher dimensional energy to solve problems in the three-dimensional world. But if the theories which I have just mentioned–Ziwu Liuzhu, the heavenly stems theory, and the acupoints and the meridians–are not being used with higher dimensional energy taken into account, their use would be limited.

The high-level Chinese medicine practitioners are those who have formed the cosmic view of "Heaven and Men Integrated as One". Therefore, treatment methods adopted by the high-level practitioners may seem odd to some people. For example, the mechanism adopted may not have a direct connection to the patients' symptoms, yet these practitioners can effectively treat illness and disease. The reason for this is that they are able to identify and deal with

61

the essence of the issue by dealing with the energies. They are able to use the energy distributed in colour, in food, in music and in space to facilitate treatments. Their treatments will not be limited to any set formula, and they could not and should not be followed and repeated in a standard way. Let me explain this point more clearly. For example, there is a point on the table, a two-dimensional plane. I can use my hand and swipe past that point on the table easily. If I were to use a stone and try to hit that same point, the possibility is uncertain. In other words, the link between higher dimensional energy and three-dimensional energy is uncertain.

The medium and high-level Chinese medicine practitioner are referred to as the "Dao Yi", Practitioners of Dao, as they are able to use or adjust the higher dimensional energy for the purpose of treatment. To adjust the images in the projection source, which is in the higher dimension, is what is known as the Technique of "Zhuyou" (祝由术). Zhuyou, the last of the 13 divisions of traditional Chinese medicine, uses the images of different energies in the projection source to achieve an offsetting result. Chinese medicine is very profound, and this is beyond the understanding of those who only possess three-dimensional knowledge. The successful treatment cases adopted by the high-level practitioners cannot be simply copied and repeated. This is very different from the western medicine approach. Western medicine, as all western science in the three-dimensional realm, is based on repetition, and requires the results to be the same in large numbers of tests. Such rigid and repetitive testing is not the practice of Chinese medicine, which would view it as an attempt of three-dimensional thought to try and manoeuvre the universal wisdom. It is a sad thing for one to use a low-dimensional wisdom to deal with high-dimensional wisdom. Even though it is true that practice is the sole criteria in testing truth, three-dimensional truth can only be tested by rules in the three-dimensional world. Low-dimensional wisdom cannot test truth in higher dimensions.

High-level dimension practices are embedded in the treatments of Chinese medicine, which is far beyond the scope of skills and techniques of our three-dimensional world. Currently, the only school of science that could understand and match the practices of Chinese medicine is Quantum Medicine. Quantum reflects the critical stage between the physical space and the higher-dimensional world, and it can reflect the energy wave and its high-dimensional nature. Modern physics has reached a very important conclusion: Quantum physics test results are influenced by the power of mind. We understand that the mind of human beings refers to those parts of energies that have not been stacked and formed into images. When we enter the fourth dimension, our super consciousness has high-dimensional energy, and the mind power energy dominates the physical energy. This is the essence of Eastern wisdom. In other words, the projection source determines the projected images. This is a very simple logic. However, if we limit our understandings to the physical world, and if we try to test the entire universe with the knowledge obtained in the three-dimensional world only, we'd be committing a mistake in logic.

We may have all encountered the mathematics problem of calculating the number of chickens and rabbits in the same cage. At the primary level, this problem seems very hard to tackle, and it is a single-dimensional operation on one axis. However, when conceived algebraically this problem becomes easy. Let the number of chickens = x, the number of rabbits = y; the total number of heads = x + y and the total number of feet of these animals = 2x + 4y. With this formula, the problem is very easy to work out. This is a typical example of solving a two-dimension problem using a single-dimension mechanism. If all two-dimension problems could be solved using the single-dimension mechanism, that would be ideal. But, so far, it is impossible. Einstein's Theory of Relativity is an exception, in which he used third-dimensional logic to solve a fourth-dimensional problem. No other person has ever done anything like this. We human beings are trying the most primitive methods to solve problems. We use algebra and apply figures in the place of actual objects. The more we do this, the more possible it is for us to find a pattern. This is the essence of mathematical experiments. In summary, the repetitive experiments, when compared with the high-dimension practices, are the primitive methods to find patterns–for example the use of statistics, and big data. The real method to conduct experiments is to enter the higher dimensions. This is the real method to solve problems.

Lecture 5 The Wisdom of Confucianism

The Heart Methods of the Secular World, and the Rule of the Game

Here are some lines quoted from the movie Lucy. "As soon as life started in the universe, they started choosing. Be immortal or reproduce. If its habitat is not sufficiently favourable or nurturing, the cell will choose immortality. If the habitat is favourable, they will choose to reproduce." Please pay attention to the word "immortality," which is a description of a state of high-dimensional energy in four-dimensional space, where time is a variant element. In our three-dimensional world, time is a constant element, measured and determined by the frequency of oscillation of quartz at the Royal Greenwich Observatory. Every second and every minute is calculated this way.

When time becomes a variant element, there is no beginning, and there is no end. In other words, in the fourth-dimensional space, there is a cycle of mortality. This is an important concept. When the environment is not suitable for a being, it will strive to improve and lift its level vertically. A breakthrough from the three-dimensional world to the four-dimensional space is achieved in the form of immortality. Two elements of great importance are embedded in traditional Chinese culture. The first element is internal, a vertical lift of freedom-of-consciousness energy, a lift in the level of dimensions. The ultimate goal is to achieve the Nth dimension (N approaches infinity). This is the level of complete enlightenment. The second element is a horizontal distribution of energy–the reproduction of a balanced, harmonious energy existence in the three-dimensional world. The vertical or hidden element is reflected by the Former Heaven Trigram (先天八卦), which deals with the concepts of time and space, as well as immortality, as its main description and aim. Vertical improvement is its form of progression. The Latter Heaven Trigram (后天八卦), of the Zhou Yi, describes a state of harmonious oscillation of energy in the three-dimensional world, a balanced and harmonious existence of energies– namely, consciousness energy and material energy.

The Confucians claimed, "One could rule the world using half of the Analects of Confucius." The first half of the book teaches us complete enlightenment. In contrast, the second half teaches us to achieve harmony between the external and internal of our body only in this limited, material, three-dimensional world.

These are the two important elements in the wisdom of Confucianism. On the surface, we can take them as the rules of the game in our three-dimensional world. These are the moderate and reasonable rules which are in accordance with the distribution of relatively harmonious energies. The backbone of these rules is enlightenment, which satisfies the ultimate purpose of life. In discussing the purpose of life, we often hear this: the purpose of life is in the improvement of the level of freedom of consciousness energy–namely, the level of dimensions, with the ultimate goal being immortality.

The root of traditional Chinese culture is Dao and De, morality (道德), commonly understood as virtue and a person's noble character. Morality comes from the wisdom of Daoism, and it reflects the inner relationship of time and space. Dao is the Nth dimensional space (N approaches infinity), while De is the presence of the levels of freedom of energy from the N-1th dimension to the fourth dimension. This is based on the saying "When Dao is lost, De remains. This is also the reason we say that the root of traditional Chinese culture is Dao and De. The ultimate goal of this culture is to improve the level of freedom of consciousness energy, to be one with Dao, by achieving the full and complete state of wisdom in the Nth dimension (N approaches infinity). In mathematics, 3: Infinity = 0; 4: Infinity = 0. Any actual figure: Infinity = 0. Only when the level is improved to the Nth dimension (N approaches infinity) could it be said that it is in unity with Dao. This is also called Heaven and Man integrated as one. This level is called the "illustrious virtue."

Here, I'd like to introduce the second concept in this lecture. In Confucianism, there is an essential classic scripture, the Great Learning 《大学》, which, at the very beginning, says, "The way of the Great Learning is to illustrate illustrious virtue; to renew the people, and only to rest upon the highest excellence." Great learning is the subject for the great, noble person, for the cultivation of thorough and complete knowledge in life. It guides the direction of the achievement of wisdom in us. The Illustrious Virtue, as mentioned before, is the purpose of the Great Learning, to achieve universal wisdom in the Nth dimension (N approaches infinity), a state of full and complete enlightenment.

To "illustrate" is to lift and raise the level of freedom of consciousness energy. In Buddhists' terms, it is called, "breaking the ignorance". What is ignorance? It is the obstacle to our understanding. To break, or to "illustrate", the ignorance is to break the obstacle to perceptions. This process is the process of achieving enlightenment. Therefore, the purpose of the Great Learning is to ultimately become enlightened with the truth of the universe.

The next part of the Great Learning is to "renew its people". One of the usual interpretations of the "renewal" is to "mix well with people"–a kind of empathy, a kind of energy. Actually, in my opinion, this renewal reflects a relationship of energy projection, i.e., the images of all beings being projected into the three-dimensional world. I have mentioned before the concept of "One Thought is One Being". When the images of the "beings" are projected into the three-dimensional world, the term "people" is being used to reflect the images. What exactly is to "renew its people"? In my opinion, it is to achieve unity between the projection source and the projected image. This enables us to directly observe in the three-dimensional world, to detect our perceptions, as our perceptions determine the images projected. This, ultimately, is the Unity of the Interior and the Exterior. In other words, all things appearing in the external world are the projection of our internal perceptions, known as "karma," in Buddhism. Therefore, the way of the Great Learning is to constantly break through our limitation of perceptions, and to achieve the Unity of the Interior and the Exterior. During this process, we examine and break through our perceptions, and we raise the level of freedom internally, unifying with Dao at the highest level.

Next comes the text, "only to rest upon the highest excellence." This highest excellence is the highest level of wisdom in the Nth dimension of the universe. The significance of the saying, "The way of the Great Learning is to illustrate illustrious virtue; to renew the people; and only to rest upon the highest excellence" is that it always talks about the current moment. The notion of the past or the future is the knowledge of the three-dimensional world. Only the current moment can enable one to improve oneself to achieve higher levels, even the Nth dimensional space (N approaches infinity), and to be guided vertically to a higher level of freedom in consciousness energy.

I'd like to describe the scientific backdrop of this definition. The single-dimension is a line. No matter how we try to describe it, it would not present any aesthetic beauty. The two-dimensional world is a plane on which we could paint a beautiful picture, N times more beautiful than a single line. The three-dimensional world is N times more beautiful than a two-dimensional plane. Through this, we could conclude that with an increase of one dimension, N times more beauty could be achieved than that in a lower-dimensional world. When we enter the fourth-dimensional world, we'd see things more beautiful than anything in the three-dimensional world. Hence, we name the fourth-dimensional world "Heaven". In my opinion, the level of "Heaven" is described as De in Daoism, and as "illustrious virtue" in the Great Learning. The purpose of life is to continuously manifest illustrious virtue expanding the dimension of consciousness energy.

When explaining his view on the purpose of life, Mr. Inamori Kazuo from Japan said, "My wish, for when the end-of-life approaches, is to have raised my soul into something even just a little purer than it was at the time of my birth." The soul is what I refer to as high-dimensional consciousness energy. The level of the soul refers to its height, its dimension. Mr. Inamori Kazuo founded two companies, which became Top 500 companies, and he rescued Japan Airlines. He also invented the Amoeba operating methods and founded Seiwajyuku, a private management school. When talking about the purpose of life, however, Mr. Inamori Kazuo didn't mention his achievements. He merely said, "My wish, for when the end-of-life approaches, is to have raised my soul into something even just a little purer than it was at the time of my birth." He's telling us that the purpose of life is to raise our level of freedom beyond the boundaries of the third dimension. This practice is related to all points of space and time that we are in at any given moment. No matter what the nature of things we are dealing with–career, love and relationships, money, or our physical body–we must bear in mind that all we do is done for the purpose of raising the level of freedom in our consciousness energy. If we don't understand this layer of the problem, we find our life meaningless and without direction.

If we study and follow the wisdom of Confucianism, using it for guidance, but not understanding its true essence, we'd be following the code of conduct on a superficial level in real-life situations. It would be a pity to have missed the true essence of Confucianism, the jewel of traditional Chinese culture, as it is not only setting out the code of conduct in the three-dimensional world, let alone merely being used, as some have claimed, by rulers to control their people. The essence of Confucianism is a cultivation method which enables everyone the chance of enlightenment in the three-dimensional world; to cultivate the mind, and to improve the level of freedom of consciousness energy. There is another important essence of Confucianism. This essence, on the inside, is linked directly to the highest level of wisdom; on the outside, it is presented as the rule of the game in reality. We call it, "To rely on the false to cultivate the true." The images in the Nth dimensional space (N approaches infinity) are being projected, dimension by dimension, into the lower dimensions, and the projected images are what I call the "false" images. The higher the dimension, the closer it is to the truth. The Nth dimension is the genuine truth. When people say, there is only one truth, it is literally quite right. When in the Nth dimensional space, all systems, all wisdoms, are integrated as one, they appear as the one and only truth. The wisdom in

Confucianism utilises the projected images and tries to lead practitioners to understand the information in the projection source, hoping to achieve ultimate truth at the highest level. This is the level of illustrating illustrious virtue until one reaches the highest level. All is done because one could "rely on the false to cultivate what is true."

Now comes the question, where does the "false" come from? In my previous lectures, I had mentioned Zhou Yi, which reflects the energy distribution in the three-dimensional world. It is also a description from enlightenment to daily lives. The ultimate purpose of human existence is enlightenment, not just for the continuation of our species. In real life, human beings often take existence in the three-dimensional world as the purpose and aim of life. This is wrong. The purpose of life is inner, vertical improvement. Three-dimensional existence is only one of the basic conditions for this vertical improvement. It is only when there is a highly harmonious distribution of consciousness energy and material energy that vertical improvement becomes possible. In other words, mind-body integration must be achieved in the three-dimensional world. If the three-dimensional world is not in harmony, internally and externally, and the internal and external are not unified, not integrated, there would never be improvement. It is futile to talk about the improvement of inner wisdom. This is what I refer to as the rule of the game in reality in the wisdom of Confucianism, which enables us to maintain a state of harmony in life. Due to the lack of this harmony, we often find entanglement in the lower-dimensional energies. Such entanglement restricts us and keeps us in the restricted world of three-dimensional knowledge. Only when we are able to enter a harmonious state of space energy, and when there is harmony between the consciousness energy and material energy in the current moment, would we be able to rid ourselves of the entanglement of the lower-dimensional energies, disentangling our consciousness from it. This is what Confucian thought has done–regulated thought to guide the code of conduct for people who are living in the three-dimensional world.

Failing to understand the significance of the guiding principles of the Confucian code of conduct, one might form a view that such code is a restriction on human behaviour, and on freedom. It is not. Materialistic attachment has turned the life of human beings into a state of hyper-materialism. Our consciousness is becoming more and more complex with the increase of our desires, and greed for more. Such complexity cannot guide us back to our original harmonious state of energy. We all know the word "man-made" is the opposite of the word "natural". When we are engaged in more and more "man-made" things, we are farther and farther away from the way of nature. In Chinese, when the two characters "man" and "made" are combined, it becomes "false" or "fake". This means, the man-made things in our daily lives are all relatively false. If this relative false is in a form of simple energy, it would be easier for us to detect the truth behind it. If it is reflected in a complex form of energy, we often become trapped by the state of complexity, and cannot see through to the truth. For example, when we spend too much time dealing with human relations, with negative personal moods, and all sorts of conflicts and entanglements, we find it hard to keep calm in our inner self and cannot ready the conditions for high-dimensional experiments.

Therefore, the "false" elements in Confucianism, or the so-called rules of the game, are for the purpose of simplifying our lives, and the relations in our lives. When relations are simplified, the purpose of life boils down to improving the level of one's inner wisdom. As a consequence, after sorting out the relations in life, each person has a chance to achieve enlightenment in their lifetime. We are all provided with the opportunity to tackle problems in life and achieve inner improvement with actual problems solved.

In 2015, when I was having a discussion on Confucianism with some scholars, I felt suddenly enlightened. I understood why Confucius wanted to restore Zhou Li, the etiquette of the Zhou dynasty. The Zhou Yi is the turning point away from the understanding of the Former Heaven system to the Latter Heaven system–specifically with regard to the theory of production, harmony and existence. In other words, the people before this turning point regarded enlightenment as their purpose of life. After that, people only regarded a code of conduct, a specific way of living based on harmony and rules in a three-dimensional world. The rules are the Zhou Li (周礼). From that time to the Warring States Period in Chinese history, people drifted more and more away from the social norms of the Zhou dynasty. That's why Confucius wanted very much to restore them, to resume the rule of games which guided people to enlightenment. When Confucius said that "at thirty I took my stand; at forty I came to be free from doubts; at fifty I understood my heavenly mandate; at sixty my ear was attuned", he was describing the process of human development and improvement in life. Of course, what he said before that was even more important: "At fifteen, I set my heart on learning." This is to say, a person should set his goal, and make a great vow of achieving enlightenment at the age of fifteen.

In the space we are in today, the most crucial thing in the heart method is faith, the faith in the self-sufficiency of all things, and that each Mass Point in the universe contains the information of the entire universe; also, the faith that any being in the universe innately owns all wisdom. Hence the saying "faith is the source of morality and virtues." Only with faith are we equipped with the prerequisite for connection with complete wisdom. Without such faith, we cannot establish the link with wisdom.

The next important point after faith is a vow. We need to have a clear goal in life. And the power generated by a vow is the driving force for all things. We may have experienced things when we were little, and we were terrified or extremely puzzled. When we grew up and looked back at those things, they seemed so trivial, and we often laughed at our naivety. This is also true when we climb a mountain. In the beginning, we'd be worried even by the height of a small hill. However, after conquering that, and after climbing to the top of an even higher mountain, the fear we had at the foot of the small mountain seems like nothing, even laughable. The great poet Du Fu (杜甫) from the Tang Dynasty wrote his famous verse, "When reaching the great peak, we hold all mountains in a single glance". On the other hand, even if we set our goal to just climb the small mountain in front of us, we may still feel the journey to be too long and eventually we might not even get there. Only when we set our goal to reach the highest peaks, will we easily pass those lower mountains swiftly and gracefully, because the vow gives us a great inner power to move forward. This is the importance of a vow. Confucius set his goal at the age of fifteen, and he succeeded. With a great vow and the power generated by it, it would be hard for one not to succeed. With a great vow, we would have more chances of succeeding. Confucius had told us of his progress and enlightenment in our three-dimensional world. Let's go through them again. The Master said, "At fifteen, I set my heart on learning." This is his vow. "At thirty, I took my stand." After 15 years of practice, he would have mastered the rules of the game. "At forty, I came to be free from doubts." Again, after ten years, he found himself at great ease in the world. "At fifty, I understood my heavenly mandate." This is because he knew his great task for this life. "At sixty, my ear was attuned." Past kindnesses and resentments have nothing to do with him anymore. He had transcended the obstacles and limitations of perceptions in the three-dimensional world and had achieved a state of thoroughness in life. Therefore, what Confucius had done throughout his life is like a teacher writing down one's personal growth in life on the blackboard for all of us.

In the past two thousand years, people have faced and solved life questions in their own way. In the time and space which we are in now, the exam questions that each of us are facing are quite different compared to the sample questions that past teachers have shown. To some extent, most exam questions are more complicated, since they are rooted in the current situation of time and space. We need to apply the essence of past sample questions into our current exam. If we are not familiar with the essence of Confucianism, we cannot give an appropriate answer to this problem of life. Let me explain it this way. If we are only following the old methods and formulas of the past and only imitate what our teachers had done in the past, we may not be able to pass the exam of current life. There is another layer of complexity here. All things in the long history experienced by people in the past—the people, the paths, the matters they dealt with—could be handled by a modern person in one month. Two thousand years ago, Jesus explained some problem-solving issues to the world. Buddha Sakyamuni and Lao Zi did the same. These issues would reappear in today's thoughts in a certain way, and we are now faced with a multiple operating maths problem. Therefore, we must try to find the commonality among these thoughts and respect their differences. These commonalities in our ancestors' wisdom can solve complicated situations based on current time and space. It would enable us to make use of current conditions to better achieve significant improvement. This is the application of Confucian wisdom. We must not merely imitate the form or the superficial part of the code of conduct. We must understand its essence, as it will assist us in our enlightenment and help us understand our inner development's prerequisite. Therefore, I say Confucianism is full of in-depth wisdom, and its application is broad. It is consistent with the wisdom in Buddhism, Daoism, and

Christianity. Confucian wisdom was developed for people in the three-dimensional world, and it does not emphasize the higher-dimensional space. It only mentions the high-level insight when mentioning the illustrious virtue in Great Learning. This is only a guide for practice in our three-dimensional world, and the core message is to "rely on the false to cultivate the truth." Therefore, Confucius said, "Attend ghosts and spirits in awe but respectfully distance them." This saying is consistent with what is being preached in Christianity, as they both do not emphasize the relationship between high-dimensional energy and spiritual energy. They both address human beings in the three-dimensional world. However, Confucius mentioned that the goal is to illustrate illustrious virtue. He pointed out the relationship between the third dimension and the Nth dimension. The Nth dimension (N approaches infinity) is the purpose of our ultimate goal in life.

Through these clarifications, we would have a correct understanding of Confucianism, whose essence is to invoke the innate wisdom in all human beings. All such forms and images are for this purpose. If we are restricted only to superficial images, we cannot be inspired by Confucianism's true wisdom.

Mr. Liu Feng

Lecture 6 The Wisdom in Theology

A Holographic Path of Enlightenment Designed for

Human Beings in the Three-dimensional World

In this lecture, we are going to discuss the relationship between theology and the scientific context. The first topic is the relationship between Genesis and theology. In Genesis, we read that God created all things in the universe in seven days. A reader would think: is this description scientific? Even though we have many modern science concepts to describe and comprehend, the reader would still be puzzled and confused. But if a reader could try to understand it using multi-dimensional space, creating the entire world in seven days becomes easy to comprehend.

There are three variants in a three-dimensional world– length, width, and height–and they can be described as the three axes of a coordinate system. In four-dimensional space, there is one extra variant: time. In his Theory of Relativity, Einstein said, when matter travels at speeds close to the speed of light, time becomes slower. Please pay attention to the word "becomes," as it is a great inspiration for us. In our three-dimensional world, time is a constant element, measured and determined by the frequency of oscillation of quartz at the Royal Greenwich Observatory. Every second and every minute is constant. When time becomes variable, there's a new variant in the coordinate system. As we know each variant defines a dimension, when we add a variable time to the three-dimensional world, we'll be entering a four-dimensional world. In this world, one could travel to the past or the future and can choose to exist in any time and space situation. According to this concept, we can understand that past and future, beginning and end, and time itself are all concepts and knowledge attached to three-dimensional space. There is no beginning of anything in the four-dimensional world, and one second could become a thousand years or a billion years, and a billion years could be compressed into one second. The concept of time being a variant is a leap in understanding of space and radically subversive. From a higher-dimensional world, one would easily and freely change, extend, or shorten the time in the three-dimensional world. Therefore, when one reads that God created the entire universe and everything in it, it could be understood that this is a description made in a higher-dimensional world. The seven days could mean seven years, or seventy years, or seven billion years. From this, I want to say that Genesis in the Old Testament is telling us that the universe is a multi-dimensional world. When time is a variant element in a space beyond the three-dimensional world, all illustrations are possible. However, suppose we only want to interpret the world using the limited knowledge built up in the three-dimensional world. In that case, we cannot comprehend how it is possible that God created the entire universe and all things in it in seven days.

In the movie "Inception", there is a very interesting interpretation of time as it plays out in different dreams or, as I'd like to put it, in different three-dimensional projections. In the movie, we see that in other time coordinates, time is defined differently. Two seconds in one space could be several minutes in a different three-dimensional space, or several hours in the next three-dimensional space, and several days in the one after. Such interpretation provides us with a key inspiration for transcending space and time. Namely, when we are in a higher-dimensional space, time is very different from what we usually perceive.

The metaphor in Genesis informs us of the simple logic that time is a variant element. The wisdom in Theology inspires us on page one to have a breakthrough in understanding time and space. However, human beings are always restricted by three-dimensional knowledge–i.e., we believe time is still a constant element, and this knowledge is our biggest obstacle in understanding the universe.

This is especially true in our understanding of things at the largest and smallest scales. The micro world is limited by our inability to divide time further. We cannot observe fundamental movements in the microworld under such limited fragmentation of time. So, we call it the electron cloud. Furthermore, we cannot provide an accurate description of the macroworld because we do not have enough measurement facility for gigantic things (approaching infinity). Things that happened 100 light-years ago are beyond our reckoning, since what happened at the time of our birth still hasn't reached us by the time of our death.

But when time is a variant element, all possibilities appear. The seven days described in Genesis could be extended to seven years, seventy years, seven billion years, or seventy billion years. As mentioned before, one second could become a thousand years or a billion years, and a billion years could be compressed into one second. All things in outer space could be brought in front of us instantly. This is the so-called Folding of Space, or the Going Through the Time Tunnel. When we can reach this level, we would not be too far away from comprehending the wisdom in Genesis.

Let us now look at the concept of the Trinity in Theology. The Trinity refers to the Father, the Son, and the Holy Spirit. What do these three terms mean in the physical world and in time and space? The Father, as God, has the universal wisdom of the Nth dimension (N approaches infinity). He is the totality of all wisdoms in the universe, the dominant figure of the universe, and the projection source of all things. The Holy Spirit is the high-dimensional energy, which is present in all places in the universe. From the Nth dimension, the projection source gets projected all the way down to the lower dimensions. The energy which exists in the entire universe, and which carries the high-dimensional information, is called the Holy Spirit. The image which appeared in our three-dimensional world is the Son, which is Jesus in Christianity.

Christianity transcends all perceptions from the fourth to the Nth dimension (N approaches infinity) and is teaching us not to attach to any perceptions in the middle. The Holy Spirit is the projection of energy from the Nth dimension (N approaches infinity). The Son, Jesus, is the projected image from the Nth dimension (N approaches infinity) in our three-dimensional world. From this perspective, Jesus is pure, and is without any defects–hence, he's called the only son of God. In the Theology wisdom system, all people are created by God, and are the projected images of God who is in the Nth dimensional world (N approaches infinity). However, because of perception obstacles at different levels, the so-called "Original sin", humans are not pure projection from the Nth dimensional world. Only Jesus is a pure projection of God in the three-dimensional world. This is why in Christianity, to go to the Kingdom of God, one must do so "in the name of Jesus". It is only through oscillating with the purest person and energy in the three-dimensional world that one can achieve oscillation with the Nth dimensional world. Any kind of energy that has a form cannot help bringing one to the Nth dimensional world (N approaches infinity). In Christianity, any form of idol worshiping in the dimensions in-between is not allowed, as one must not try to achieve oscillation with energies in-between.

The Holy Trinity is in high consistency with the Triple Jewels or Triple Gems in Buddhism. They are called the Buddha, the Dharma, and the Sangha. They can help explain the Holy Trinity and vice versa; they verify each other. The Buddha represents the universal energy and wisdom in the Nth dimension. The Dharma is the energy, which is connecting all energies in the universe, while the Sangha is the projected image in the three-dimensional world. Of course, there are differences between the descriptions of the Son in Christianity and the Sangha in Buddhism. In Christianity, the Son is a pure body of energy which is a direct projection of energy from the Nth dimensional space (N approaches infinity). In Buddhism, the Sangha is the embodiment of the Buddha, and should in theory be a pure body of energy. However, since it is a person, he has a certain level of obstacle in perception. Therefore, Sangha does not have the purity that is represented in Jesus, even though, Buddha Sakyamuni appeared in our three-dimensional world with great pure energy. In conclusion, I'd like to point out that different religions can verify each other, even though there are some minor discrepancies in the descriptions.

Now let's talk about the sacred scripture in Christianity, the Holy Bible. The translation in Chinese is Sheng Jing, the "sacred sutra". The Bible is a heavenly book, as it is a book which comes from the higher dimension. All sutras, or classics, or sacred scriptures come from the higher dimensions. They were projected and appeared in our three-dimensional world and are written down by people who are in contact with the high-dimensional world. It is like a downloading of high-dimensional energy.

The sacred text of the Bible obtained through the above-mentioned method is very profound. People of different times in history or at different times of their own life, would read and comprehend different levels of its messages. A

Christians who read the same section of the Bible at different times, in different locations, or with a different context, would have different experiences. The texts, which are the projected images from the Nth-dimensional world (N approaches infinity), are interpreted according to the level of perception of the reader. A reader of limited knowledge in a limited dimension could only achieve the perception at its corresponding dimension level.

Dao De Jing, the Daoist Classic, is the same. When it is applied to explaining the human body, nature, or political problems, it will have all the correct answers, as it comes from the highest-dimensional projection source.

About a decade ago, there was a popular book, The Bible Code, written by American journalist Michael Drosnin, who wrote this novel based on the technique described in the paper "Equidistant Letter Sequences in the Book of Genesis" by Professor Eliyahu Rips of Hebrew University in Israel with Doron Witztum and Yoav Rosenberg. Prof Rips is famous for his studies in geometric group theory. In his book, Drosnin describes an alleged "Bible code", in which messages are encoded in the Hebrew bible. The messages are purported to be hidden in the Torah and can be deciphered by placing the letters of various Torah passages at equal intervals in a text that has been formatted to fit inside a graph. By entering the name Yitzhak Rabin, a former prime minister of Israel, in the graph, Drosnin found the expression "assassin who will assassinate". He was shocked by this, and he approached Rabin's guards. However, Rabin did not take note. One year later, Rabin was assassinated. Drosnin went and checked the graph carefully again. This time, he found the name Tel Aviv, which is the location where Rabin was killed, and Amir, the name of the assassin. Even the time of the assassination was indicated.

However, no such prediction would emanate when using such a method with classic books like War and Peace or Anna Karenina. This is an important indication to us that the Bible is a multi-dimensional holographic information system. When we apply different coding or techniques to interpret, different information emanates from it. The time and space which corresponds with the different information is related to the time and space of our current world.

This is why we need to be peaceful when reading the Bible, and why we must use our heart to sense, respond, and resonate with it, rather than merely read the text superficially. The text of the Bible has limitless interpretations. The more we read it, the more our consciousness resonates and oscillates with it, the more we are able to understand the inner meaning of the Bible. Chanting the Bible would be more helpful than reading alone to foster this resonance and oscillation. When our eyes are in contact with the Bible text, which is the projected image from a higher dimensional world, our vision would be under the power of the Bible. When we read the text aloud, our hearing would be under the influence of the Bible. If we lit incense, our sense of smell would be under the power of the Bible. When we focus our energy at the "dan tian" (丹田), the lower abdomen, our entire body, would oscillate, accordingly, putting our sense of touch under the power of the Bible. And then, when our mind is under the power of the Bible, our holographic power would be awakened. Therefore, the reading and chanting of the Bible is a way of both practicing and cultivating this holographic power as well as a means to awakening this power. The deeper we try to understand and comprehend the Bible, the more we will be blessed by its higher-dimensional energy and be oscillated by its power.

The Bible itself contains all information, and it all depends on what kind of code we use to comprehend the information. I had purchased the second edition of the Bible Code, and I was once again greatly inspired by it. The multidimensional and holographic nature of the Bible has inspirational insights with respect to the past, present, and future. If we were only to understand the Bible from its stories, we would not be able to comprehend the subtlety of its connection with the high-dimensional power of the Bible. Only when we could see through the surface, and calmly oscillate with it, would we be able to understand the true essence in it.

There are two essential elements in the wisdom of Christian theology. The first is love and the other is the transcending of death. These are the two most important heart methods designed for practical human beings. In three-dimensional space, the strongest energy we can feel is love. This is highly consistent with teachings in other religions. Modern psychology and psychics also strongly emphasize that the most fundamental existence in the universe is love.

We are in a three-dimensional world in the solar system. The incredible energy we feel is the sun. Therefore, the sun is a representation of love. What does the sun signify? Give. The sun is constant: it shines and gives unceasingly, without seeking reciprocation. This is the essence of love. Therefore, love is the truth only when giving. And genuine love is our greatest joy, happiness, and satisfaction. We all have this kind of life experience when we genuinely love someone; at the moment of giving love, we feel the world is terrific, and we are filled with joy and satisfaction. However, if we start to have the thought, is he or she loving us, too? Our happiness disappears. Therefore, only in a state of pure devotion can there be the genuine beauty of love. Since the sun seeks no reciprocation, it is the essence of genuine love. While the sun does not seek reciprocation, the spirit of its love is reflected in its relationship with the Earth, since the reception of nutrition from the sun also requires total devotion, indiscriminate devotion. The reception of love is achieved at the moment of devotion. The sun would not give extra heat because one person is good; it would not give less heat because one person is terrible. The sun does not discriminate. The love of the sun is indiscriminate. All religion emphasizes this type of great love.

Christians believe that God loves all people. Due to the three-dimensional cognition limitation, people tend to seek love from others, from the outside. If we are able to truly believe God is in you, and God is with you, we would easily understand the teachings that the Buddha also says–that all sentient beings have the innate wisdom of a Tathagata, and each being is intrinsically self-sufficient. When we realize that each being has full and complete inner wisdom, each body would be the emanater of love, as well as the noumenon of love. When one is the emanater and the noumenon of love, and is intrinsically self-sufficient, one is functioning as devotion, and would not require reciprocation.

Insofar as we in three-dimensional space are attached to the material level of energy, we would be only seeking love, and seeking it externally. Some might believe that their capacity (innate or otherwise) to attract love has transcended their need to seek love. Actually, attracting love and seeking love are the same, insofar as they are both external behaviours. Only when one believes in the intrinsically sufficient self, and in God's presence within oneself, would one understand oneself as love. Wherever one is, there is love, as one is always with God.

Light is the same. Most people are afraid of darkness, and they seek light involuntarily. Some people strive to become a superstar, chasing the limelight. But those who understand the truth of the universe understand that each entity is intrinsically self-sufficient, and each person is a light source. In the presence of light, there is no darkness, as light shines on all things. Darkness appears only as an obstacle to, not a co-existent with, light's presence. This obstacle, in the sense of one's cognition, is whatever blocks our truest understanding. When we take away the obstacle, darkness disappears. Therefore, the truest understanding, God loves the world, reveals the logical structure of Christian wisdom in Theology as the truth of the universe.

There are two essential elements in the wisdom of Christian theology. The first is love and the other is the transcending of death, also known as the transcending of life. Three days after Jesus's crucifixion, he rose from death. This is also a very important heart method. People in the three-dimensional world attach to the idea of life and death--therefore, death became their biggest fear. While Jesus's own bodily revival counters the absolute status of death, the deeper understanding of his resurrection applies to all beings: as long as we enter the spiritual life, we won't die.

What is the status of spirit? Spirit belongs to the higher dimension. As we could see in the movie Lucy, "As soon as life started in the universe, they started choosing. Be immortal or reproduce. If their habitat is not sufficiently favorable or nurturing, the cells will choose immortality. If the habitat is favorable, they will choose to reproduce." The word "immortality" means the development and improvement of one's life to the higher dimension, from the third to the fourth dimension. Spiritual life is of great importance to Christianity, as it is the link between life in the three-dimensional world and the higher dimensional wisdom. To return to God's kingdom, it is a transcending of life and death. This echoes exactly the definition of life and death in the Dao De Jing, the Daoist classic. Coming out of life and entering death is a commonplace phrase in the Chinese language. Coming out of life means the projection of an image from a higher-dimensional space to a lower-dimensional world. Entering death is to return to the projection source. The ultimate origin of all things in the universe is the Nth-dimensional space (N approaches infinity). That space is called God's kingdom. Therefore, in Christianity, life comes from God's kingdom, and all return there. Another saying in the Chinese language, death is a return, describes the same message. In Buddhism, it is called reincarnation. Therefore, on the issue of life and death, the wisdom in theology has provided us with two very important inspirations.

In Christianity, there is an essential ritual–baptism, and an essential related teaching, Original Sin, which baptism is believed to absolve. In Buddhism, the understanding of sin is called karma, the full understanding of which transcends the three-dimensional world. In the three-dimensional space in Christianity, sin is something that comes with the self. As long as we are human beings, we would have such understanding. Otherwise, we wouldn't be projected as human beings in this world. In Buddhism, the understanding of sin is accumulated through many, many lifetimes. In Christianity, it is something that hinders the connection between our inner knowledge and the higher dimensions, up to the Nth dimension of God. Baptism is a cleansing. The current situation of our life is like a mess. Even if we add a little to it, or erase a little bit, it wouldn't make any fundamental difference. However, baptism cleanses us entirely. After baptism, we are like a clean sheet of paper. Not that we who have been baptized will not ever sin again. It's just that it will now be easier for us to notice our sin, or error, as a mark on a clean sheet of paper. This visibility increases our capacity to reflect upon all our behaviour and thought, thereby increasing our capacity to connect with God.

The practice of Christianity is a heart method. When describing the universe, it is applying the heart method. It tells us that, if we attach to any dimension from the fourth dimension to the Nth dimension (N approaches infinity), we would be restricted by our own thoughts. In such a situation, we would never be close to the Nth dimension, to the real wisdom and enlightenment, and we would not be able to make connection with God. The sole purpose of our life is to enter God's kingdom, which is the Nth dimension, the realm and state of enlightenment. Only life in this dimension would truly and completely be full and perfect. That is the sole purpose of life, and all religions are pointing to this same goal.

Lecture 7 The Wisdom of Spiritual Systems

The Integration of Psychics and Spirit

When we human beings analyse different wisdom systems, we tend to neglect the limitations of the default system in which we are conducting the comparison and criticism. When the subject of the discussion is religious wisdom, psychic or spiritual wisdom, many people habitually apply scientific thinking and logic to criticize those wisdoms. As repeatedly mentioned in the previous lectures, under the prevailing environment of empirical science, we human beings often make the mistake of attempting to solve high-dimensional problems with low-dimensional methods.

Let's now have a look at the psychology system. To date, the relatively authoritative method in this field is Sigmund Freud's psychoanalysis. Why? Freud had used ample clinical psychoanalytic tests or statistics conducted in the three-dimensional world. Such three-dimensional knowledge is a strong support for his theory. What exactly is psychology? In my opinion, psychology is the study of the consciousness activities of a person. We have already shown that consciousness, in essence, is a kind of high-dimensional energy. There is no difference, in nature, between this kind of energy and the energy in the physical world. Indeed, the physical world itself is formed by these overlapping energies. However, when associating consciousness activities and the physical world, psychologists haven't been able to form a set of theories supported by modern, scientific logic systems; they merely separated psychology from the modern scientific maths and logic system. But in my opinion, they can be linked up logically.

The nature of all matter is the energy wave, which forms two different kinds of matter in the three-dimensional world. The first is mass—the objects which result from the overlapping of energy. The other is consciousness, or information, thought included. The Yi Jing has 64 trigrams which are formed by stacking the basic 8 trigrams onto each other. The 64 trigrams represent the distribution of energy and the basic information of the distribution. The 64 trigrams are the fundamental genes of all things in the three-dimensional world. The so-called genes are the spectrums which record the stacking of energies. When these 64 basic spectrums are stacked together, millions and millions of things are formed. Please note that all matter is included in these things. Matter, which is the information of the mass objects or "things" involved, are all part of the consciousness activities of human beings. In other words, consciousness activities and physical activities are all results of the stacking, or overlapping, of energy waves, and these are all connected in the three-dimensional world. At this stage, no research has covered the level of the interchanging relationship among these things. The change happens at the quantum state.

Modern physics lab tests prove the link between the result and the consciousness of the experimenters. This gives us a very important insight: Change in the physical world is associated with the consciousness of man. Change in a physical object is associated with our consciousness. Knowing this, when we re-examine this theory system, we can feel like we are enlightened. In other words, in a three-dimensional physical world, the energy waves form objects and the information about the objects; in a four-dimensional world, the energy waves still exist, yet the energy is of a higher dimension, and it is called the sub-consciousness. Sub-consciousness is the energy distributed underneath the surface. What is the relationship between the energy distribution of sub-consciousness and our reality? From the logic system mentioned before, we understand the relationship is of a projection source in a higher dimension and the projected images in a lower dimension.

Actually, psychology is a study of the interface relationship between the third and fourth dimensions. It does not analyse from the quantum perspective, nor from the maths perspective. It comes from the consciousness perspective. It analyses the relationship between consciousness in the third dimension and consciousness in a higher dimension. Let's talk about psychoanalysis, a term which comes from The Interpretation of Dreams by Sigmund Freud. It is a study of the preconsciousness. What is a dream? The nature of a dream is a high dimensional issue. For example, if we take a nap after lunch, and we have a dream, we might feel the dream to be very long, but when we wake up, we may find that only 5 minutes have elapsed. A lot of people also have this experience: The contents of their dream do not follow a chronological order. The scenes in the dream are different from reality, and the measurements of time in different dreams are also different.

Through contrasting different dreams, the movie Inception illustrates brilliantly that "time is a variant element." Whenever time is a variant element, the fourth dimension appears, one dimension more that the third-dimension. Dreams belong to the higher dimensions–minimally the fourth dimension. Some people have experiences like this: When they go to a strange place, they feel the place to be very familiar. However, after they awake, they realize that they couldn't have been there before. Why is this? Actually, they might have been to this place before in their dreams. Because, in the dream's fourth-dimensional world, time is a variant element. Moreover, one can go to any point of time on the time axis, including the future. If you had been to a place in the future in your dream, and later you actually go to the place in the three-dimensional world, you've felt the familiarity–the, at first, mysterious familiarity, sometimes referred to as deja vu. The interpretation of a dream is achieved through analyzing its relation to what has happened in the three-dimensional world, to find out the internal reasons in the projection source, and then to provide guidance and adjustment, etc.

Part of psychology deals with cognition, which is cognitive psychology, and it fits well with the system we are describing, in which the actual world we are seeing is formed by our cognition. When talking about the mathematic models of Yi Jing in the Daoist wisdom, I specifically talked about the importance of the third energy wave. This third energy wave is an energy wave which has been rendered or projected onto the hologram by an observer. This energy wave comes from us, the observer, who carries a unique spectrum which is actually our cognition. In other words, our cognition, our understanding, determines what images are rendered and projected onto the external world. As we explore further in the study of psychology, we see that more and more psychological methods engage higher dimensional consciousness. Let's take hypnosis for example. This is a method to bring someone out of the restricted three-dimensional world, and take him to an expanded three-dimensional space, by maintaining the links between the images in both three-dimensional spaces. The ability of hypnotherapists varies. Most don't have the ability to bring out the things that happened before this lifetime. Most can only trace back to some hidden things in present lifetime memory. But there are notable exceptions. Dr. Brian Weiss is a famous doctor, and also a hypnotherapist in America. He has written four books on so-called "past-life regressions". The first book is called Many Lives, Many Masters.

Catherine, Dr. Weiss's patient, came to him to treat her various problems, or phobias, such as, fear of darkness, water, being choked by food, and interacting and communicating with others. Initially, under Dr. Weiss's hypnosis treatment, when she was able to think of her past, there were no incidents that could plausibly account for the cause of her fear. However, Dr. Weiss was adamant that in hypnosis treatment, one must be able to return to the point of time, in current or in past life, when such triggering events happened. By so doing, the patient would be able to resume cognition from that point of time and re-engage the event. As a result, the patient would be able to dissolve the mental entanglement and obstacle. After his initial set-back with Catherine, Dr. Weiss tried some deeper hypnosis with her, and she said something after the treatment which shocked the doctor. Catherine said, her consciousness went back as far as the 1500s, in a place in France. Dr. Weiss had not expected Catherine would be able to relive what she had experienced in her past life. He had expected her to experience something in her current life. Hence, he continued to guide her to try and find out what had happened. In that lifetime, there was a flooding in the village Catherine lived in. She and her mother were both drowned. This is the reason Catherine is fearful of water now. After some struggling on the treatment chair, Catherine calmed down. This hypnosis treatment was a great turning point in Dr. Weiss's practice. He later had many other findings, which will not be introduced here. Dr Weiss struggled, too, as to whether to publish the findings of his treatments. He was an atheist, and he didn't believe in any religion, nor in reincarnation. To believers in the logic system of western medicine, all these sound ridiculous. However, he totally believed in the theories of psychology he applied in his practice, so he eventually decided to publish the findings of his treatments. In further past-life treatments, he uncovered many hidden guidance. For example, in one of her past lives, Catherine was in

Russia and was in the form of a seven-year-old boy. His father was wrongly sentenced to death, and she couldn't stand the torture of such cruelty, and she died soon after. During a break in the treatment, Catherine's voice became very deep, like that of a male. The male's voice asked Dr. Weiss, do you know what I had learned from this incident? Dr. Weiss was shocked, but the male said, in this lifetime he had come to learn that no one should be wronged. Dr. Weiss later learned each of us is here to finish our homework for this lifetime. How could that be achieved? By choice! If one chose to be a poor person, or a rich person, or be a king, he needs to achieve his goal. To love. To accept. To forgive. To embrace all. We must learn from this invisible "master" (as in Many Lives, Many Masters). This master, as I put it, is the spirit in a higher dimension, a high ego in modern spiritual studies. In Chinese culture, they are referred to as the original spirits, or the spiritual consciousness. They represent the energy relationship of the projection source in the higher dimensions. It will establish connections under special circumstances with energy in the three-dimensional world.

Hypnotherapy can lift a person from the three-dimensional world to the fourth-dimensional space, which is the higher projection source. When in this higher dimension, all three-dimensional worlds look equal. It's like if I stand in the centre of a room, the four walls can be seen by me. If I were to put my focus on, and be attached only to, one wall, I would have less or no sense or consciousness of the other three walls. Hypnotherapy is a method for one to be able to see in different three-dimensional worlds the different projections of the same projection source, and then, make changes. With this understanding, we do not need to rely on hypnosis in our self-cultivation. In other words, we don't need to know the relationship between our past life and our current life. We only need to go to the projection source to make all the changes, as all images in the three-dimensional world come from the fourth-dimensional space. By comparing the different images in different three-dimensional worlds, we would eventually come to face the relationship as reflected in the fourth-dimensional space, which is the source, and the origin. Once the entanglement at the source has been dealt with, the problems in the lower dimensions could be easily transcended. This is the theory of hypnotherapy.

In recent years, there is another popular stream of psychology treatment - Family Constellation. Two basic theories are being applied in this method: universal holography and the adjustment of the four-dimensional projection source–i.e., to changing the projection source to achieve different images in the projection. During Family Constellation therapy, a teacher guides a group of students in role-playing. The students are to play the role of a family member, and to adjust their energy to suit that role, in the hope of achieving a correct understanding of the relationship among the members, and to achieve a resolution.

Why does role-playing by a couple of people have an effect on the real situations of a family? The Family Constellations method is in accordance with the Law of Universal Holography. A random mass point in the universe contains all the information about the universe, and the connections among all the information. We can extend this concept. Each person contains all the information about the universe, and the connections among the indefinite points in it. In other words, you, and I, have all the information, and energy, all the time and in all places. And, my interpretation of the word "possession" actually means that some innate energy within our body becomes active, and manifests under some specific instructions. During the Family Constellation role-play, different students play different members of the family–the father, the mother, etc., and the teacher. The instructor, based on their feelings and senses, assigns the students to be at certain locations. They are encouraged to have interactions, and the instructor modifies the energy field through their interactions. Why could simply anyone be chosen to play the role of a father, a mother, etc.? Because any person has in them the holographic information of a father, a mother–in fact, of anyone. When we are in the right energy field, and have totally let ourselves go, we can, under a specific instruction, utilise the information within ourselves, and render the energy of that information.

There is one important precondition to this treatment – the students must obey the rules set by the teacher, the instructor. If a student opposes this process, and is reluctant or rebellious toward it, the effect would be greatly discounted, even if he participated in the treatment, because this treatment requires a holographic approach. The requirement for the instructor is that he must have the higher-dimensional vision. If not, things will be difficult. The person under treatment can be lifted to a dimension as high as that of the instructor and start to become energy entangled. If the instructor could not control the situation, it would be like he had unzipped a bag and could not zip it back closed. This could be dangerous. Family Constellation treatment utilises holographic information and introduces consciousness to the projection source. Each of the participants lets go of their role in the three-dimensional world, and enters the higher dimension of the projection source, in which the energies are changed, and then re-projected into the three-dimensional world. When this is achieved, the reality in the three-dimensional world changes too. This is the fundamental theory behind this treatment. However, such treatment, like hypnosis, can be very dangerous. Opening the source code and source programs of ourselves to an instructor, or a hypnotherapist, makes us more vulnerable to both harmful and helpful instruction and treatment.

In recent times, Super Psychology, or Spiritual Depth Psychology, transcends the relationship between the third and the fourth dimensions, and enters another deeper sphere–super-consciousness-which is related to awakening. The fundamental aim of traditional psychology is to solve problems. For super psychology, the aim is to awaken wisdom in a person. In recent years, many traditional practitioners have turned to super psychology. More and more attention has been paid to spiritual development, as human beings are now on the track of moving from the third dimension to the higher dimensions.

Super psychology is very interesting. When modern scientists, grounded in three-dimensional logical thinking, expand their dimensional boundaries, they remain clinging to attachments–for example, a constellation in the universe, a status of a level of space, or the image of a grand master, etc. Such attachments more or less hinder the link between them and the ultimate complete wisdom. I once had a discussion with a person in charge of a super psychology program. He said in his programs and classes that he had always allowed the participants to experience their spiritual status. I said, spirituality is something of higher dimension, and allowing people to experience the higher dimension status is dangerous. He then realized his results were in agreement with this caution. As it turned out, many participants felt happy during the programs and classes; but, when the program was over, they felt exhausted, sick of society, and needing to run away from reality. They became attached to the programs and classes and wanted to participate in programs or classes all the time. He then asked for my suggestion. I said, genuine spiritual classes should provide a guidance which aims at the highest dimension, instead of merely experiencing and dwelling at a certain dimension which is not the highest dimension. A program should emphasize the power of the vow. The purpose of the great vow is aiming for the Nth dimensional universe (N approaches infinity). I will be covering this topic in future lectures.

Any super psychology system must have an ultimate back bone which supports the system, and that is the thorough awakening of wisdom. This ultimate backbone is enlightenment. But as long as one has attachments, one is hindered from cultivating it. When we look at the Diamond Sutra, we read that Sariputra asked the Buddha a question, "in what should a virtuous man or a virtuous woman abide in, and how should they subdue their minds?" The essence of the question is on how to subdue the mind. Buddha Sakyamuni replied, "for a virtuous man or a virtuous woman who has already generated the mind of Anuttara-samyak-sambodhi, he should abide as such, and should subjugate his mind as such." When one has generated a great vow to achieve the complete, unsurpassed, and perfect enlightenment, he should put his mind to the Nth dimensional universe (N approaches infinity), which is the ultimate aim of all spiritual cultivations. This should be the only direction. If one dwells in a certain level of dimension, he would be restricted, and would hinder himself in his pursuit of full enlightenment.

When different religions or spiritual systems describe different high dimensional spaces, they have different ways of describing, and their level of understanding is manifested in their descriptions. It's like when someone is cutting a full cake. Thin slices or thick slices? Vertical cuts, or horizontal cuts? These are not important–the essence, the cake, is of importance. In Buddhism, there are many different levels of heaven–for example the heaven of Mahabrahmana, Trayastrimsa, Tsuti, Nirmaarati, Parinirmita-vasavartin, etc. In the Kryon system, there are eight levels, which means eight energy levels. In the Law of One, there are various levels, and they are described in densities. Let me use The Law of One as an example and explain.

In the Law of One, a group of scientists tried to make contact with higher-dimensional, extra-terrestrial wisdoms. They didn't rely on any "scientific" methods. Instead, they used a medium who could connect with these higher-dimensional beings. The medium would lie on the bed. On a bench close to the head, there would be a crystal ball, and incense, etc. The scientists would ask questions and the medium would answer. The answers were all written down, and they were very abstract and difficult to understand. The medium entered a higher dimension and described the life situations there. He tried to provide answers to the three-dimensional questions asked by the scientists in the three-dimensional world. And the answers given by the medium are very interesting. For example, the scientists asked, "What form are you in", and "Where are you from?" The medium answered, there are eight densities in the universe, and human beings are in the third density. The medium was in contact with the fifth or the sixth density. The scientists then asked if he had had any contact with humankind? He said yes, back in the times of the pyramids. The scientists then asked what he had done when he made that contact. The medium said, they helped the people build the pyramids. As to how, he said, with the power of the mind. The scientists asked, if he was able to do that with the power of the mind, why didn't they build the pyramid in one piece, instead of stacking blocks and blocks of large stones. The reply was that that would be unacceptable to human beings. The method must be one that could be accepted by human beings at that time. What was the purpose of building the pyramids? A pyramid is a collector of energy from the universe. Those who live in the pyramid could receive high dimensional energy from the universe. Later they stopped building pyramids, because they found that human beings were very selfish. The medium said the pyramids were built to serve all people on earth, yet the Egyptians only used it for the pharaohs. This is one of the sessions the scientists recorded.

The scientists also asked, how long are human beings going to stay at the third density? The medium was very cautious and precise in his answer. He said, human beings are supposed to be in the third density for 75,000 years, which is divided into three equal stages. At the conclusion of the first stage, no spirit was mature enough for them to harvest. At the conclusion of the second stage, some spirits were mature enough, yet they chose to stay on earth. They were those eminent monks, sages and saints, who chose to stay to help advance the spiritual life of human beings. At the conclusion of the third stage, all human beings would experience a common lift. What stage are we in now? The medium said, we are at the end of the third stage. We have thirty years before the end of the stage. When the experiment was conducted, it was 1981. So, 2011 and 2012 would be the turning point between the third density and the fourth density. At this time, the inner consciousness energy has turned from three-dimensional status to a higher-dimensional one. Before that, we paid more attention to material needs. After this point, we attach more importance to spiritual and high-dimensional things. According to the Mayan calendar, the end of the world would come in 2012. Actually, that was not meant to be the end of the world. It was the progress of the human beings' lift in the level of dimensions. It was the end of a three-dimensional cognition, and it was to be a transcendence. We are now in the time and space where higher-dimensional energy is in dominance. This is a Dharma-ending period for the third-dimensional era. In the fourth-dimensional space we have entered, human beings are gradually becoming self-enlightening.

Therefore, we should all aim at entering the highest spiritual sphere, which is the Nth dimension (N approaches infinity) by self-cultivation. Some may ask, if all aims for, and goes to, the Nth dimension, what would be left in the three-dimensional world? But the third dimension and the Nth dimension are just descriptions. Dimensional spaces are not external worlds. The dimensions lie within. All the external matter we see is the projection of the inner mind. The high-dimensional space is within. You can't find it without. In the Heart Sutra, the eminent Bodhisattva's name is Guan Zi Zai. Guan means "to reflect inwardly". To reflect that the presence of self-nature is great ease. Great ease is the situation of the Nth dimension (N approaches infinity). "Presence" refers to the current energy status. It describes our lived inner consciousness, including beyond death. Such description of energies, and the commonality of, and the commonalities between, such descriptions, reflect that the essence of life is to be found in consciousness energy, and the purpose of life is to improve its level of freedom. Emptiness of a space doesn't mean empty of meaning or significance. Some say that the lower dimensions would disappear. There is no such issue. We, as human beings, are not concerned too much with what's happening to ants, whether they are fighting with each other, or whether their nest is empty. This is a description of the view from a higher-dimensional space. It is like in the Heart Sutra, where we read, "When Bodhisattva Avalokiteshvara practices the profound paramita..." What is "paramita"? It is the deep dhyana concentration, the entering deeply into the high-dimensional space. When the dimension is high enough, he looks back and "perceives that even the five aggregates are empty of intrinsic existence." The lower-dimension worlds, which are not solid and concrete, are void in nature, and they are intrinsically self-sufficient, and they cannot be attached. The ultimate point of the highest-dimensional world is the Nth dimension (N approaches infinity). I want to emphasize again, this is not the ultimate truth, and this is only one description. But we can rely on this description to help us understand all cultivation methods that are used.

Lecture 8 The Science Wisdom System

The Past, Present and Future of the Development of the Human Science Civilization

In this lecture, I'll tap into the core topic of this lecture series – science logic, or what I have called the Science Wisdom System. All the systems I have talked about in our human world are descriptions of different wisdom systems. Each description has its own complete logic system and is self-consistent. The Science Wisdom System is a complete logic system whose origins date back to early human history. It describes the existence of the three-dimensional world, and the connections among all things in it. Human beings have been trying to provide a complete description of all the things themselves, too. With the development of science, we have gradually come to an understanding that there are many unknown things about the world that are beyond our exploration. In other words, the way of thinking that is science logic is limited to practical activities in our three-dimensional world, with the eyes, ear, tongue and body as exploring utilities, and this is how the system of science wisdom has been established. Through these methods we have a better and objective understanding of

113

the world. Now, let me give a summary of the past, present, and future of the development of human science civilization.

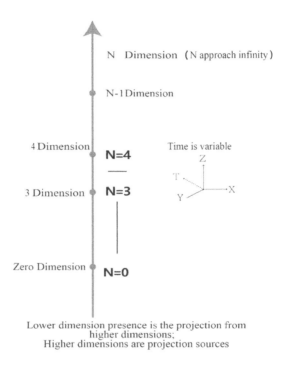

Figure 11 Multi-dimensional space illustration

Let us begin by revisiting the logic framework of the entire system, which enables us to understand the connection between our intellectual system and other systems, and to explore the possibility of the limitless extension of its self-consistency. The first concept of reality to explore in this framework is the concept of space. The concept of linear geometry was used to explain the universe from the 0th dimension to the Nth dimension (N approaches infinity). The concept of space is used to completely dissect the entire universe, and to strictly describe its logical relationships. In other words, space is big with no bigger space on the outside, and it is also small yet with no smaller space inside. The second concept of our framework reality derives directly from our explorations of the wisdoms in space–the method of finding the commonality among all wisdoms. Through this method, we know that the commonality among all existence is molecules. In other words, it is molecules that form matter. To explore further, the commonality among molecules is an atom, as atoms form a molecule. An atom is composed of a nucleus and one or more electrons. Nuclei differ, but all electrons are the same. A nucleus is composed of one or more protons and a number of neutrons, which is the commonality. A proton is composed of neutrons and positrons (positive electrons). After going through such analysis, we've come to an understanding that there are only three basic matters: neutron, positron, and negative electron, all of which are referred to as elementary particles. The commonality among these three particles is their quantum property. The quantum property is the wave-particle duality. The commonality of the wave-particle duality is the energy wave. When the wave forms the interferometric imaging of a standing wave in space, we can see its existence. This is called the "particle nature". Those parts that did not form any images kept their wave nature and formed relevant information and consciousness. Therefore, wave nature is the commonality of all existence in the entire three-dimensional world.

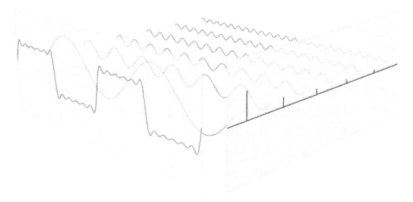

Figure 12 Illustration of Fourier Transformation

In reality, there are many different kinds of waves. The Fourier Equation tells us that all energy waves can be described by means of stacking Sine waves–in other words, all things can eventually be described in the form of Sine waves. Therefore, the Sine wave is the most elementary existent in all the descriptions of our logic system, which means the most elementary existence in our universe is the Sine wave. The stacking of Sine waves is the basis of all existence in our world. When analysing Sine waves in our three-dimensional world, the focus has been on the amplitude and the frequency; but another very important element has been neglected. When we combine one more element–space–we find that the dimension of the energy wave is much more important than the amplitude and the frequency.

The relationship between different energies in different dimensions is the relation of projection source and

116

projected images. Therefore, the Nth-dimensional space (N approaches infinity) is the projection source of all things in the universe. With the understanding of this projection relationship, we'd understand the relationship of energy distribution in the entire universe–i.e., the relationship of the projection of energy waves. In the transmission of energy waves, we've learned another concept--that any one mass point in the universe contains all information in the universe, and all connections among all information. In other words, each energy wave would go through this mass point, even though this point might not only be small, but have no smaller particles on the inside. This is the law of cosmic holography. Buddha Sakyamuni said, "All sentient beings have the innate wisdom of the Tathagata, and each being is intrinsically self-sufficient." When a Daoist says, "Dao is present all the time, in all places," they mean the same, and when a Christian says the same about God, this is the core of their wisdom. Using this core information, we are able to find that there is a connection in all the wisdom systems. When we search for the commonality amongst the differences of all wisdom systems, we can see that they are highly consistent in their teachings and can verify each other at a very high level.

Today, even with the accelerating evolution of science and technology in our world, most worldly scientific descriptions are readily seen to be rooted in the three-dimensional world, especially on authoritative issues where principles have been established based on practices in the three-dimensional world. These principles, after being recognized, established and tested, are all true, as practice is the sole criteria in testing truth. However, three-dimensional truth can only be tested by rules and principles in the three-dimensional world. When examining things in the higher dimensional worlds, it is a logical error to use such principles. Do higher-dimensional worlds exist? All the wisdom systems we have encountered so far are revealing to us that, apart from the world in which we are living, there are other higher dimensional worlds. In those higher dimensions, there would definitely be other forms of descriptions, and there are many, many things that are beyond the scope of so-called modern science in our world.

When we are open to such a thought, and when we expand the science domain from the three-dimensional world to the Nth-dimensional space, and we look back at the connections among all wisdom systems, we find that they could verify each other. Such verifications would make it easier for us to better understand the entire universe, and to thoroughly understand and comprehensively approve all the wisdom systems.

I. The Accumulation and Passing Down of Human Knowledge – The Limitation and Passing Down of Three-dimensional Practices

We, as human beings, have always held a view that today's knowledge system and the science and technology system are a result of many years of accumulation. Is the knowledge correct? It is, of course, in our three-dimensional world. It has been recognised, tested, and eventually established as the formal knowledge system underlying all human science. Each invention has gone through a lot of facts and experiments. Such is the process of accumulation. However, what exactly is knowledge and perception? Where do they come from? For most people, statistics and accumulated knowledge are of great value, as they come from real practice and original creativity. Yet, where did the original thought come from that drove all these practices? What are the driving forces of all these originalities? From the relationship between projection source and projected images, we understand all creations come from spiritual inspiration.

The word "spirit" could be understood as a higher dimension. The spirit, or soul, is high-dimensional energy. Spiritual inspirations come from information in the high-dimensional world. This thought is itself inspiring: initial thoughts of all scientific experiments come from the high-dimensional realm within. Inspiration drove all the tests and experiments which, with further statistics, eventually led to the establishment of knowledge. There is another scenario. People of high-dimensional abilities were able to download information from the higher-dimensional world, and created a wisdom system, which was then disseminated and propagated. During the process of propagation, those who had the abilities to download the high-dimensional information did not merely pass on the knowledge, or information–they were able to *integrate* the knowledge and wisdom.

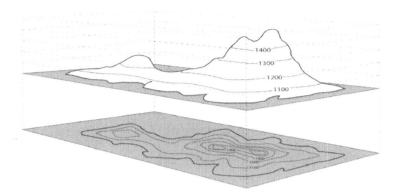

Figure 13 Contour lines illustration

Let me give you an example. We can project a three-dimensional image of a mountain onto a two-dimensional plane, in the form of contour lines. These lines are the so-called knowledge. The actual mountain is the source and is the wisdom. A teacher who teaches his students to search for the mountain is a teacher that is conveying the Dao. Those who teach the contour lines are teaching knowledge, but those who impart the relationship between the contour lines and the mountain are both teaching knowledge and resolving confusion. Thus, a teacher who seeks to convey the Dao, impart knowledge, and resolve confusion will explain the high-dimensional information through the two-dimensional descriptions, thereby inspiring his students to understand high-dimensional wisdom. The two-dimensional descriptions are but a tool to explain the relationship between the two- and three-dimensional world.

120

Knowledge has been used as yeast–a stimulant for inducing wisdom.

However, what if a student had not established the ability to search for the mountain, and the teacher departs from the world, leaving the student only the knowledge on the contour lines? Then, after becoming a teacher, this student could only teach the traditional contour lines in such a way: The small circle is the top of a mountain, the largest one is the bottom ring of a mountain. Where the lines are close, that's an indication of a cliff; where the lines are widely apart, that's an indication of a gentle slope. However expertly this teacher could read and explain the contour lines to his students, trying to explain what a mountain was, he was actually not describing the real mountain. He would only be describing some lines on a two-dimensional plane. In other words, he had imported knowledge only. Furthermore, what this teacher had taught might not have been the absolute truth. When a student learns the so-called contour lines, he cannot go further and research the mountain. This is the limitation we are facing. This limitation of understanding hinders the perception of the entire universe.

What is the biggest obstacle in the perception of our three-dimensional world? It is the limitation of the three-dimensional world and knowledge. In the three-dimensional world, there are only length, width and height, with time being the constant element. However, as Einstein has told us, when the speed of an object approaches the speed of light, time becomes a variant element. Under this circumstance, the fourth dimension emerges, and none of the four elements could be definite. Time, the fourth element, which is important in the three-dimensional space, becomes unimportant. Clinging to a three-dimensional world understanding, unable to comprehend that time is a variant element, is the biggest obstacle to our perception in the three-dimensional world, especially with respect to the most extreme ranges of the micro and macro world.

Our understanding of the micro world is limited by the inability to further divide time. Under such limited fragmentation of time, we are not able to describe the movements–namely, the electron cloud–in the micro world. So, too, due to the fact that we do not have enough measurement facility for gigantic things (approaching infinity), we cannot provide a proper description of the macro world, as things that happened 100 light years ago are not relevant to us. What happens 100 light years away at the time of our birth will not have reached us by the time of our death. This is why the biggest obstacle to perception in our three-dimensional world is the perception that time is a constant element. This topic has been discussed in the Diamond Sutra, where it reads, "Neither the past, the present nor the future mind can be found." This is because the past, the present, and the future are all forms of time. When we are restricted in perception, time is a constant element and there is a distinction of such different time forms. How, then, could we manage to be connected to the higher dimensional world? The current moment! When we are truly living in the current moment we would be connected to the Nth-dimension (N approaches infinity). The "form of a life" mentioned in the Diamond Sutra is also the form of time. Only when we surpass such forms would we be able to enter the high dimensions.

However, due to strong and stubborn belief, human beings limit their understanding to the three-dimensional world, and, as a result, we have a wrong understanding of life and death. The fear of death makes human beings uncertain of their soul after they die. Such limitation in the three-dimensional world spurs us to accumulate more knowledge, and to strive for more prosperity. How do these help to improve the meaning of life? In fact, they become the biggest obstacle, as mentioned before. We cannot grasp all the information that is in the entirety of the three-dimensional world, because we are only focusing on this single dimension. We are not paying attention to any point outside this dimension. Such perception truly hinders the development of our logical thinking. In the two-dimensional world, although we are able to include points other than those that are on one line, we are still not able to grasp all the information in the entire two-dimensional world, as it is immeasurable. In the three-dimensional world, there are far more possibilities, enabling us to create immeasurable knowledge and complex information, and thereby create real prosperity for our lives. All scientific knowledge is the result of the stacking of information, the stacking of energy relationships of existence. When these energies are presented in different forms in the three-dimensional world, the reproduction of information makes the three-dimensional world even more complex. However, it is this complexity that hinders our connection with the higher-dimensional world.

Why, then, must we try and achieve a higher dimension? This is a very simple concept. In the single-dimensional world, there is no beauty to mention. In the two-dimensional world, a picture is endless times more beautiful than the line, which is the entire single-dimensional world. In the same way, a three-dimensional object is endless times more beautiful than a picture in a two-dimensional world. In short, we can understand that, with the increase of one dimension, there are endless times more beauty, and one more level of freedom. Such freedom could lift us to both a great joy and a great relaxation. The energy in the higher dimension is the projection source of the images projected in the lower dimension. Therefore, in a higher-dimensional world we'd have a better control of life. The lift and improvement of the level of freedom in consciousness energy is the sole purpose of life. With the above-mentioned backdrop, all information and prosperity in the lower dimensions become insignificant. Therefore, if we were to cling to the limitation of perception in the three-dimensional world, our improvement would be hindered, and we would not be able to achieve intrinsically perfect wisdom.

Up to now, all the advancements in science and technology in our world, when compared with the wisdoms in the higher dimensions, seem very limited. Why? Even though there are endless lines in a two-dimensional plane, even though there are endless planes in a three-dimensional world, there are endless cubes in a four-dimensional world. No matter how much information or how great the prosperity in the three-dimensional world, when compared with the fourth-dimensional world, the comparison is 1: infinity. The same applies to the comparison with the fifth. In other words, the achievements and knowledge in the three-dimensional world could be considered trivial when compared with the entire universe. If we were to cling to the limited perception of knowledge in the three-dimensional world, we'd hinder our own improvement in understanding the entire universe. When we understand this point, we understand the most fundamental insight: any one mass point in the universe contains all the information in the universe, as well as the connections among all information. Through this we know that each person in the universe is intrinsically self-sufficient, containing all information in the universe, and the connections among all information. In fact, each person is in high consistency with the Nth-dimensional universe (N approaches infinity) and is intrinsically self-sufficient with respect to all possibilities.

Given the above-mentioned conditions, why are we not able to live in a situation which realizes a complete and intrinsically self-sufficient life status? It is because of our limited and restricted perceptions. Our level of understanding and perception confines us to that level of life status. When we are restricted to three-dimensional thinking, we are restricted to living in the three-dimensional world. Those who are living in the three-dimensional world yet are able to travel between different dimensions and make connections between them, are able to implement and carry out the essence of the higher-dimensions in the three-dimensional world. Such inter-dimensional adepts are referred to as the "internal sage, external king" in traditional Chinese culture.

From the above descriptions, it would not be difficult for us to understand that however much the development of science and technology brings improvement and growth, such improvement and growth can hinder our capacity to transcend the three-dimensional world by increasingly restricting our perceptions. When one lives in the three-dimensional world, one can still use its limited knowledge to awaken the limitless wisdom within one's self. By using the knowledge as yeast, or an enzyme to grow and to expand internal wisdom, one could be awakened to one's own wisdom. It all depends on how one treats this knowledge: to look up from a lower position, and regard knowledge as the dominion; or to look down from a higher position, or from the same level, and use knowledge as a tool that could inspire wisdom. The former would make you a slave of knowledge, while the latter would enable you to control, and create new knowledge. We human beings have endless creativity, because we are all intrinsically self-sufficient, and there is no reason that we should become a slave to knowledge. At this stage of development in our society, we are able to store nearly all information in the cloud. In other words, if we want to acquire knowledge, we could get from cloud storage whatever is needed for our purpose.

As we increase the functions and capabilities of robots, and the robots are connected to the cloud storage, it could be disastrous for us. If the majority of human beings are not able to be connected with the cloud and make use of the knowledge available there, they could become slaves to the robots. Such results have already been predicted by western scientists. Robots today which are supported by knowledge available from the cloud already have an intelligence that is equivalent to a three-year old. What is there to stop robots from surpassing human beings in their grasp of knowledge in the not-too-distant future?

There is good news, however, in that we, human beings, have entered a new era, an era which initiates a progression from the three-dimensional world to the higher-dimensional spaces. In other words, the majority of people on earth are seeking growth in spirituality–that is, an improvement in the perception of higher dimensions. Such perception is categorically higher than that in the cloud. Spiritually-based science, which surpasses current science, is called Universal-Point Technology. Universal-Point points to the Nth dimension (N approaches infinity). Through internal cultivation and practice, one can return to one's inner wisdom, which would be categorically higher than that in the cloud. One would be able to control the universe– namely, time and space. If we were to only dwell in three-dimensional knowledge, we'd be left far behind, as all things in the three-dimensional world are showing signs of destruction and decay. All natural and man-made disasters are warning us–urging us–to embrace the need to break away from the three-dimensional world and seek the higher dimensions.

Accessing such higher knowledge would clear the fear of the "formation, existence, destruction, emptiness" of all things in the three-dimensional world. Why? In the higher-dimensional world, we are intrinsically self-sufficient in all possibilities. But if we don't lift the three-dimensional perception to a higher dimension, we remain fearful. Currently, all businesses, careers, all life situations– pollution, the economy, wars, are sources of fear and emotional entanglement. However, we can lift ourselves from this situation by realizing all these decaying signs as warnings to us to improve our level of wisdom.

II. The Two Forces for Development in Human Civilization – The Pursuit of Eternity and The Fulfilling of Desires.

Looking at the history of China, we can see that attachment to three-dimensional reproduction and development began in the time of the Zhou dynasty. Before the Zhou dynasty, the conduct of morality and etiquette was preconditioned by the goal of enlightenment. The Former Heavenly Eight Diagrams, the *Yi Jing* Theory of time and space, indicated enlightenment as the foundation for human beings. Eternity was the purpose of life at that time. From *Zhou Yi*, the *Yi Jing* of the Zhou dynasty, we can see that people started to pursue a complexity brought forth by the energies in three-dimensional materials. When such complexity matched perfectly the internal consciousness energy, and created a harmony in the energies of consciousness and materials, a new set of rules was created, and it was called the Etiquette of the Zhou. When the Zhou dynasty collapsed, the Spring and Autumn period started, followed by the Warring States period. During such tumultuous times, Confucius saw the underlying problem. He realized that attachment to desire and greed in human beings was far greater than it was in the time of the Zhou dynasty, and that people had gotten farther and farther away from enlightenment. At this time of disintegration, Confucius advocated the restoration of the Etiquette of the Zhou in the hope that all could return to following the rules of the game, and return to the pursuit of enlightenment.

There are always two lines of development in humanity and a horizontal reproduction and expansion. In the *Yi Jing*, the text of the Trigram of Qian says, "Heaven is in motion ceaselessly. A noble person exerts himself constantly." Heaven's motion refers to the higher dimensions. A noble person's constant effort means that only through great effort can one enter the higher dimensions, into the projection source. It is through internal improvement that one lifts his levels and becomes enlightened. The text of the Trigram of Kun says, "the Earth is supportive of all. A noble person with great virtue bears the utmost." These two trigrams describe two directions of cultivation, vertical and horizontal. These two directions are the essence of all cultivation and improvement, with the vertical improvement being the ultimate purpose.

In the classic texts which have been passed down to us by our ancestors, and also in other texts of wisdom in other cultures, we can see the two parts of wisdom, the "implicit" and the "explicit". The implicit part is the part that inspires enlightenment, which is for our cultivation, our spiritual improvement, and internal progress. While the explicit part is the part that governs our conduct in a beneficial way, enabling us to live well, with great ease and dignity. To find the essence in all civilizations and wisdom systems is to be filled with "Dharma joy," because of the improvement and lift. We can also be fulfilled in the explicit life form in our society in the full and complete sense. The explicit and the implicit forms coexist in harmony and complement each other. One is the projection source and the other is the projected image. The improvement in the source will enable higher and better images in the projections. Therefore, the improvement in the source is the fundamental improvement, and the pursuit of eternity is the ultimate pursuit.

What is the contradiction in reality? The desire for, and attachment to, the three-dimensional world. In other words, the attempt to retain the complexity of the three-dimensional world, and the attempt to realize its so-called joy and happiness. This is a big misunderstanding, as the driving force behind this is desire. Desire is the feeling of lack. One is always thinking that he needs more. With such mentality, one would always be following the cycle of "formation, existence, destruction, emptiness" of all things in the three-dimensional world.

How many times have the civilizations in our world been destroyed? Lemuria, Atlantis… Why? Because this is the normal rule of "formation, existence, destruction, emptiness". All things formed must be unformed eventually. Destruction is the natural course. What does the latest destruction teach us? This should serve like a whip, an encouragement for us to improve to higher and higher levels of dimension, and thereby assist the joint improvement of humanity. Without such mentality, we are in constant fear and anxiety in our life, like a burning inferno.

In our traditional Chinese culture, the concept of "the Dao follows nature" is a very important one. Nature is in full harmony with the Dao. What is the opposite of Nature? Man-made. In the Chinese language, the word "man" combines with the word "action / make," and forms the word "fake" (伪), or "false". All things in the three-dimensional world, no matter how complex, are images from the projection source in a higher dimension. If we cling to the projected images, we can't find the genuine connection between the images and the source. Therefore, with each invention in science and technology, there comes from heaven, or the universe, a warning: such development and improvement is against the Dao, against Nature. If we could try and understand it from this perspective, we would truly begin to consider: should the direction of scientific development be towards technology, or should it be towards the true and comprehensive understanding, and even enlightenment? I think this should be the dominant direction of the development of human science and civilization.

What is culture? Culture is the explicit representation of energy in the three-dimensional world. What is civilization? Civilization is the explicit representation of the level of achievement. It is explained in the saying, "The way of the Great Learning is to illustrate illustrious virtue." The civilization is the illustration of the level of perception. The perception is the projected images in a three-dimensional world of a source in the higher dimension. When we can enter a higher dimension, we can manifest a higher level of civilization. Currently, human beings regard the civilization of the three-dimensional world as a prosperous civilization, and I'd say, this is a wrong perception. Our ancestors had told us long ago that, "the way of the Great Learning is to illustrate illustrious virtue". We need to continuously improve the level of our dimension, and strive towards the Dao all the time. We need to lift our level vertically to higher dimensions.

Vertical improvement is no doubt a difficult path, based on the Universal-Point Technology. But one of our technologies is a powerful tool to assist us. The ubiquitous Internet technology has torn apart the boundary between the third dimension and the higher dimensions. The basis of development in Internet technology is the speed of calculation of our computers, which exceeds the restricted and limited perception of time and space, and which enables the modelling of progress that is impossible to map in our current world. The current perception of space and time in our three-dimensional world has been broken through, but that is only a first step. Our progress in the compression of the speed of time hasn't done much for a breakthrough in dimensions. Most scientists have based their studies and research for the truth on three-dimensional thoughts, and their methodology is thus always on incorrect ground. The wisdom systems for the Asian are different. We tend to have a holographic view of the entire universe, and we search for the truth from the view from the top. Through such structure and perspective, we could build a true science and a true civilization for the future of human beings. Such science would include all information in the third dimension, all scientific theories and laws; at the same time, such science would include infinite space, and help pave the way for our consciousness to enter limitless civilization.

III. Transformation and Transcendence of Science – Holistic and Holographic Universal Views

The Holistic Universal View means the view that all things in the universe are integrated as one. This view enables us to see the one essential truth: all things happening in the universe are connected.

In the reality of our three-dimensional world, most people understand our world from a lower, restricted viewpoint, especially in recent times, when commercial civilization has made us attach too much importance to the value of things, resulting in a price tag for all things. We have completely been dominated by, and saturated in, the commercial mentality, judging people even by their material assets. When we use this same principle on the world, economic development, the cumulative GDP of all countries, becomes our prime yardstick. But if we try to apply the same yardstick to the universe, we would be stuck, as we cannot put a price tag on a star, the Milky Way, or the galaxy. The construction of a Universal View, by contrast, is to take "Heaven and Man as One". We need the base of the universal view to establish our worldview; the base of our worldview to establish our life view; and only then establish our views on value. This is the optimal universal energy link–for the projection source to determine the projected images. Seeking the higher dimensional source of projected images enables us to find the true meaning and purpose of life. To live out the true significance of life, is to live out its truest happiness and joy, as well as its greatest glory and value.

Now, let's have a look at the Law of Holography of the Universe. When we treat the entire universe as one entity, there is actually a pivot point–namely, a mass point in the universe that contains all the information in the universe, as well as the connections among all information. This is the Law of Holography of the Universe, and it contains the theory that the universe is big yet with no bigger space on the outside, and that the universe is also small yet with no smaller particles on the inside. It is the view of "Heaven and Man Integrated as One", and the Dao's presence at any time and in anywhere, forming the noumenon of life, in which the universe and we are integrated as one. All the presence in front of us is merely the illustration of our internal entanglement of universal energy. The projected images form all the images in the universe, from the single dimension to the Nth-dimension (N approaches infinity). The Buddhism wisdom is able to comprehensively illustrate these images, as the Surangama Sutra presents us with all the detailed descriptions and classifications, from which we could see the reason why human beings are human beings, and nature is nature, and all the connections whereby human consciousness has evolved to its current complexity.

Therefore, the concept of energy enables us to find out what responding level one has achieved. This is called transformation and transcendence. With such a concept, one is able to integrate all wisdoms in our world without creating any conflicts among them. Such integration could inspire greater interest in accessing innate wisdom. In other words, to open up to our intrinsically self-sufficient wisdom. Let us not blindly follow any one method, or any one grand master, or any one collection of sayings. Let us be, rather, in a state of intrinsic self-sufficiency, in which any methods, ways, theories or wisdoms would be of assistance in our development and cultivation. For a true practitioner, all things are integrated as one. The entire universe is one entity. It's only due to different levels of perception that we appear otherwise.

The use of Universal-Point Technology is to inspire all mankind towards a status of integration and completeness, ensuring the fullest internal connection between the self and the current moment. All wisdoms belong to the current moment. The relaxedness, joy, and happiness of the current moment is truly meaningful in one's life.

In this lecture, I have covered the past, present, and future of the scientific development of human beings. Eventually, all in the universe will be integrated as one, consistent with the essence of all religions. Therefore, there is no conflict between science and religion, as the development of science can lead to our enlightenment. But science does not just mean science in the three-dimensional world. It also means the scientific logic that reaches all the way to the Nth-dimension. This enables us to understand the link between all the human wisdom systems.

Lecture 9 The Ecological Wisdom System

Vertical and Horizontal Ecological Systems and Sustainable Existence and Development for Human Beings

I. The Eastern Interpretation of Ecological Wisdom Systems – The Vertical Ecological Chain

When the word "ecology" is mentioned, most people think of "environment", the "ecological environment" around us. I'd like to extend the definition to the "state of life". When we look at the "state of life" from the perspective of the entirety of the universe, and we combine "state of life" with the entirety of traditional Chinese culture, it wouldn't be hard for us to find a vertical ecological chain, which includes the states of life of the universe, nature, energy, society, and humanity. The state of life of the universe is beyond the three-dimensional world, and it is connected with our heart.

Many years ago, when I was engaged in environmental protection, my expertise was in solar power. I found that if we advocated for environmental protection along with economic growth, the former would be the excuse for the latter, and it would be difficult to achieve the target of environmental protection. Indeed, for many years now, although environmental projection has been a key concept around the world, our environment has nonetheless been repeatedly damaged. Therefore, I proposed a simple concept, "spiritual environmental protection"–that is, the state of life of the universe. From the fourth to the Nth dimensions (N approaches infinity), in the "integration of multicultural systems", there is a collection of all the information of all the knowledge we've acquired internally. In Buddhism, this is called the Alaya Consciousness. The information that exists internally within us projects all the various levels of the states of life. At the same time, the description of the Nth-dimensional universe is a description within the entire universe. This is why I name it the state of life of the universe.

When the state of life of the universe is projected into our three-dimensional world, we call it the state of life of nature. Projected images appear in the three-dimensional world due to the relatively balanced interference of energies. This is the reason that we can see all the different things in our world – the natural and healthy balance of energies, and the diseases and natural disasters. The state of life of nature is connected to all things.

We should pay attention to one thing above all in the state of life of nature–that is, the state of life of energy. Human beings living on our planet need to use resources stored in the earth to sustain our lives. The biggest and most important resource that comes from the earth, and that supports life, is energy. However, when examining the ultimate source of energy on earth, we understand that all energy comes from the sun, which then gets converted into all sorts of energies on earth. The state of life of energy is a direct reflection of how we, human beings, make use of the resources on earth. If this state of life is damaged, there is imbalance on earth, leading to natural disasters.

Then, there is the state of life of society, which is the harmonious relationship of the energies of social interactions. When studying the state of life of nature and energy, we need to also consider the influence of this state of life of society, as it, too, contributes to the state of life of the entire universe. Let me give you an example. In the past, when we were trying to restore the natural ecological system of a mountain area, we might have taken some drastic measures, such as sealing off entire areas, and moving all the native residents out, providing them with subsidies. But in doing so, we would have ignored something critical. Those native residents in the mountain areas had been living in the mountains for generations, and their lives were closely connected with everything in the mountains. When they were moved away, they might get a subsidy in money, but when they used up the money, they would start to become burdens for the local government, as they would have lost their ability to live self-sustainably, as they had in the mountains. When they descend into poverty, they become one of the elements of social instability and imbalance. Therefore, when studying real-life ecological systems, we must also consider the balance of the state of life of society. Otherwise, our entire energy system could also be damaged.

Now, let's turn to the state of life of humanity. The exchanges and clashes among all cultures are all important exchanges of energies. In the past few millennia, different cultures appeared in different locations and in different ethnic groups. With the development and expansion of information and migration more frictions and clashes appeared. These were due to the strong, independent elements in the cultures that could not tolerate the similarly natured elements in other cultures. We have learned of many such cultural clashes throughout history. Therefore, the state of life of humanity, of culture, is another important part in energy relations, and must not be ignored.

These five states of life–the universe, nature, energy, society, and humanity–form a vertical ecological chain from which we could conclude that the entire universe is of one entity. An imbalance in any of these five states affects the entire chain, the entire system. We could also come to realize that the state of life is actually Dao, which is everywhere at any time. Take, for example, the state of life of civilization. The state of life of civilization is De. At the very beginning of an important classic scripture, the Great Learning, it says, "The way of the Great Learning is to illustrate illustrious virtue." "Illustrious virtue" is the Dao. To illustrate virtue is to improve and lift the level of dimension, and the illustration is the civilization. What is the definition of civilization? It is the level of consciousness of human beings. And the expression of the state of life of civilization is De. In Dao De Jing, it says, "When Dao is lost, there is De left." The departure from the Nth-dimension (N approaches infinity) is the entrance to the N-1th dimension. From there to the fourth-dimension, all are descriptions of De.

What is the responsibility one should assume under a certain state of life? By responsibility I mean a restriction that is commonly agreed upon but is not regulated by law or precepts. In other words, it could be understood as the "heavenly law". Whenever the word "law" is mentioned, most people think of restrictions. However, heavenly law restrictions are pledged and undertaken by all members and entities of a society for the protection, and love, of that society. There is a difference in examining environmental issues from a single perspective and from a holistic perspective, as the holographic perspective comes with heaven and man integrated as one, containing information of the entire universe as well as the connections among all information. Such harmony is the harmony among energies in the entire universe, manifesting the harmony among the entire consciousness, and also the harmony of energies between consciousness and matter. It is the true healthy state of human energy.

Through the above discussions, we can understand the rich contents of the state of life. In other words, we can understand that the state of life is not limited to environmental protection. It includes the society, the culture, humanity, and also the four views as mentioned by President Xi Jinping.

The first of the four views are the "universal view that we believe in: harmony between man and nature". This means, as mentioned before in the lectures, "heaven and man integrated as one", and all wisdoms in the universe integrated as one. This means, infinity: infinity, and the result is 1. When our internal wisdom has extended to the Nth dimensional universe (N approaches infinity), and has integrated with the universe as one, such formula would work. Such "one" is the genuine "one," with "heaven and man integrated as one", everywhere and at any time. Just like the Dao. Just like God. From this perspective we can say that the "universal view that we believe in harmony between man and nature" is the true noumenon of the universe.

The second view is the "international view that we value peace and harmony in state-to-state relations." There are many states, or countries, in the world, with different geography and resources. These states are an integral aspect of the three-dimensional world in which we live, and, their overall state of harmony is based on the third–namely the "social view that we uphold the principle of harmony without uniformity". Such non-uniform harmony is a full balance, and the optimal oscillation of different mentalities, ideologies and coexistences. This, then, leads to the fourth view, "the moral view which cherishes harmony and benevolence in our ethics". The fourth view is consistent with the universal view, as Dao is the Nth dimension (N approaches infinity), and the moral view is the universal view. Morality is the description of all different levels of energies in the universe. This is the root of Chinese culture, whose essence is the culture of virtue, the virtue of the entire universal culture, and the holographic universal culture.

In the current space we are living in, and from this perspective, we can see that the leader of China has delivered a full and scientific description of the entire system. If we could understand this point, we would be able to understand that the vertical state of life includes the energy relations in the entire universe.

II. The Macro Stages of Human Existence and Development – Primitive Coexistence, Savage Competitive Survival, Civilized Competitive Survival, and Harmonious Coexistence

Let's take a look at the horizontal development lines of energy, matter and human history. After living beings emerged on our planet, and after human beings came into existence, we went through a couple of very distinct stages.

The first was the Primitive Coexistence stage. During this period, human beings had no need to exploit the earth's resources. The resources on the earth were sufficient for all. At the same time, human beings were living in a way that was in accordance with the earth, with nature, and with the entire chain of the states of life. That was the reasonable existence of human beings on earth at that time, and there was harmony between man and nature.

With the growth of desires, human beings wanted to access more and more resources, and have more rights. At this time, we entered the second stage, the Savage Competitive Survival stage. At this stage, the weak were at the mercy of the strong, who invaded and looted whatever they wanted– mainly the resources of the weak. Under this pretext, human

143

beings went through a disastrous stage of development, with on-going wars, killing and looting, and all sorts of hatred as a result.

After the two World Wars, most human beings came to the realization that, if this trend were to be continued, human beings would vanish, long before the earth's natural use-by date. Nuclear war alone threatens ultimate mass distinction. With this in mind, some people started to put their focus on mitigating the excesses of predatory economic activities. The development of concern for a more balanced world economy was a shift from the looting of resources of the past to a more civilized distribution. This indicated the coming of the third stage–the Civilized Competitive Survival stage. With the development of commercial and financial activities, human beings achieved a significant redistribution of resources and wealth. However, one of the most important elements has been neglected–the over-exploitation of the earth's resources. We have come to realize that we have created a huge conflict between ourselves and the earth. A lot of places on the earth are no longer suitable for use; water and ground sources have become contaminated, as has the very air we breathe. It increasingly seems that, even before the sun dies out, we will have nowhere to reside.

During the stage of development for economic prosperity, we had used all possible talent to drive the progress and took this as a sign of advancement in human civilization. This was actually a big mistake. From the perspective of universal energy harmony, the only natural energy relationship is one that is healthy and sustainable. As we've come to see, the Dao follows nature. And the opposite of nature is "man-made". What conclusion should we draw from this? We should understand that no matter how well and how complex we make the images of this three-dimensional world, there is not much significance in it. The most significant thing to do is to make the connection with the higher dimensions by breaking through the obstacles between us and the higher-dimensional energies. All developments in science and technology may be a good thing in what they had set out to do, but they will also bring unknown catastrophe to human beings. The ancient Chinese who were full of wisdom had reminded us that advancement in technology is not the best thing, and they understood, from a high-dimensional perspective, that human beings could be the victims of the extreme pursuit of technology.

Without this understanding, we might not be able to realize the true situation of our competitive survival: we are drinking poison to quench our thirst. The over-exploitation of the earth has seen many overdrafts on the future resources which belong to our children and their children. We see that, in order to stimulate the economy, many different tricks have been applied. For example, the "Double 11" (November 11th) Online Shopping Gala has been promoted to stimulate sales, which, as a result, leads to a lot of impulsive buying and spending. While the increased sales boost helps the manufacturers to stay in business, it also creates a lot of waste, using up limited and precious resources. People who spend their money impulsively seldom have a proper use for the products they buy. The resultant waste is yet another overdraft of the earth's resources. Such overdrafts are the inevitable result of an economy-oriented development that considers consequences only as an afterthought.

This situation is like the relationship between the front wheels and the rear wheels of a car. The rear wheels will never catch up with the front wheels. The front wheels are the development, and the rear wheels are the environment and responsibilities. What's worse, the rear wheels will never be able to make up for the damage created by the front wheels. The reason that we see more and more efforts put into environmental protection these days is our recognition of the devastation caused by our front wheel drive. At this present moment, we must change our mentality entirely by changing the nature of the wheels. The front wheels need to be named responsibility and become the leading force for sustainable development. You may notice that we hear less often the phrase "sustainable development," as we are now facing a bigger problem–a survival crisis.

It is my hope that human beings will be able to enter the fourth stage of development–Harmonious Coexistence among all people, ethnic groups and countries. There should be great harmony among us all. Such harmony would be complete, holographic, and totally natural. It would be the existence of harmony between consciousness energy and material energy. This is the future which we should all aspire to.

III. The Essence of the Wisdom of the State of Life – High-level harmony between consciousness energy and material energy.

High-level harmony between consciousness energy and material energy matches one of the descriptions of communism: abundance in materials and improvement of ideological awareness. In the modern history of the West, there have also been enlightened capitalists promoting great abundance in materials and improvement of ideological awareness. Therefore, enlightened capitalists and communists have chosen the same path in this respect. Buddhists who believe in the Pure Land of Bodhisattva Maitre, and a "pure land on earth", are also advocating this same high-level harmony between consciousness energy and material energy at this moment of time, at this moment of reality.

The essence of state-of-life wisdom is to achieve harmony at this moment in time. This creates a big challenge for all of us. The world we are seeing now is a reflection of whether we have harmony within our heart, within our mind. As the Buddhists have said, "all phenomena are the creation of the mind", and everything is the projected images of our internal perception. When the internal world is in great harmony, the world we see is beautiful and in harmony. However, now, at this very moment of time, are we able to see through the descriptions and find their organizing essence? This organizing essence underlies all existence in the three-dimensional world, all of which is subject to the natural stages of "formation, existence, destruction, emptiness". Why? Because all the movements of energies in the universe underlie all the forms, which are subject to the four stages described above. This is a description of all things in the three-dimensional world, where time is a constant element. In this world, the initial interferences were rather weak. When the interference is strong, the images would be very sharp and clear. Later the images will become more and more vague, before they disappear eventually.

In fact, all matter in our world must go through the stages of "formation, existence, destruction, emptiness", with different presentations of destruction and emptiness.

Our natural environment, our social and international environment, are all deteriorating at an accelerating rate, with more and more natural and man-made disasters. Is there any true significance in our discussing environmental protection in this context? Yes. And it's straightforward. The discussions are indispensable to lifting the level of freedom in consciousness in order to achieve transformation; both for the evolution of the energy of all human beings, and for entering into the higher-dimensional space of consciousness. Nonetheless, we need to understand that the destruction of the three-dimensional world is definitely coming, and we need to distinguish between trying our best to grasp hold of every minute and every second of our limited lifespan, and trying to lift our existence, surpassing our limited perception–especially that of the three-dimensional world–and to eliminate our attachment to the material world, departing from commerce-oriented social behaviour, and entering into, by taking responsibility for, the vertical energy relationship. We need to put our life into the high-dimensional energy cycle, a vertical cycle in which we could truly lift ourselves into a higher-dimensional world. If we remain restricted to our three-dimensional world attachment, we will see our own demise in the stages of "formation, existence, destruction, emptiness". Such ongoing attachment will lead to fear, and a state of living worse than death.

In this lecture, I have talked about the wisdom of the state of life, which includes the environment, our entire outer universe, as well as the internal universe within us. At the same time, it also includes our society and the reality of our world. All these are encompassed by the complete holographic universe, which provides the holographic view of the state of life. This fullest view is what would give us the fullest confidence in the future of human beings.

Lecture 10 A Symphony of Life Composed by Many Wisdoms

I. The Spatio-temporal Properties of Life – Life in Multi-dimensional Space

We in the three-dimensional world have a very clear and correct understanding of the essence of life–that is, the inevitable process from birth to death. Despite this same process for all, each life is unique. Some live a happy life, while some suffer, even enduring great disasters. In a previous lecture, I had talked about Dr Weiss' book Many Lives, Many Masters, which describes many different lives which were the projections of different minds of past lives.

Actually, to many people, the process of life in this three-dimensional space is unknown, and is mysterious to them, as they do not know what to expect tomorrow, let alone the long-term future. Such unpredictability is regretful in life. However, when we view life from a higher dimension, a lot of things which seemed to be impossible, or to have

151

happened in a random manner, are seen to have actually been meant to be, or destined to be, that way. For example, if there is a light source projected onto a wall, and if I put my open palm in between, a shadow, the shape of my palm, would appear on the wall. If one is on that two-dimensional wall, and tries to trace the outline of the palm, and started from where my thumb is, s/he wouldn't know what would be coming next. However, when viewed from the three-dimensional space, away from the wall, one could easily see the whole picture on the two-dimensional wall. The same applies to lives in the three-dimensional world when viewed from a higher-dimensional space. The whole picture, and the whole process of life, would be very clear from the four-dimensional world. what is to happen and when in one's life is clear, and is destined. Why so? All images and things in the three-dimensional world are projections from the source in the higher-dimensional space. This is described in Buddhism as "yuan", " 缘 ", destiny, condition or connection. In Buddhism, there is neither a beginning nor an end to a life. It speaks only of yuan, a conditioned origination. All things in the three-dimensional world are destined by the projection source in the fourth-dimensional world.

Just as we understand the term "conditioned origination" through its descriptions in Buddhism, we can also understand another of its concepts, "reincarnation," the continuity between past, present and future lives. Various images that appear in the single-dimensional world to be scattered and isolated, will all appear to be connected in the higher-dimensional space. Each image in the three-dimensional world is part of the past, present and future life, and is like a dream. Life does not exist in the three-dimensional world alone. There are many, many higher dimensions, which cannot be understood by people in the three-dimensional world. However, from the perspective of a high point of the universe–the perspective found in the ancient wisdom of our ancestors–we can understand the levels of all kinds of lives–levels that our ancestors have clearly described. When we, from a lower position, try to look and search for the truth in the higher levels, we cannot figure out the truth. Only when we have a holistic view from the entire universe, are we able to see all things and lives evolved, and the significance within.

Let's return to the wisdom of Daoism. When discussing life and death, Daoists use the terms "Chu Sheng" (出生 out of life) and "Ru Si" (入死 into death). What do they mean? Out of life means a life that has just come out of the womb of its mother. What does "into death" mean? If we apply the concept of projection and projection source, we'd understand that "into death" means a life that returns to the projection source. In this way, we are able to understand the Buddhist term "Wang Sheng" (go and be born, or reborn), and Going Home, "treat death like returning home".

When describing life, the Christians say, God created Adam in the three-dimensional world, and took a rib from Adam and created Eve. Please note, Adam was made out of earth. What is earth? Earth is a composite energy in the three-dimensional world as a result of two-dimensional energy oscillation and interference. Since earth contains some other energy elements in it, the nature of Adam's descendants could be said to be intrinsically constituted of the same Five Elements of Daoism. From Adam's body, God took a rib, which contained all information in relation to Adam. This shows that it is the overlapping and interferences of two information frequencies that creates life. In China, Fu Xi and Nu Wa are the symbols of these energies. The origin of life could be described as an integration of Sine Wave energies, a collection of energies. In Christianity, as described in Genesis, the universe begins; and then human beings were created; and then the human race started to grow, and the entire civilization evolved. There is a very important concept here–i.e., human beings live in the three-dimensional world, and God is in the Nth-dimensional space (N approaches infinity). In between, there are endless dimensions, which we human beings cling to too tightly. The Christian heart method is that all human beings should strive to leave the three-dimensional space and try to arrive at the Nth-dimensional space (N approaches infinity), where God is. Do not cling to the dimensions in between. There is another important concept that God is in everyone. God is with you all the time. This describes the entirety of the universe, and also the energy relationship between life and high-dimensional space.

Through all the wisdom systems, it is not hard for us to see that there are actually many levels of dimensions. We can describe them using mathematical logic. For example, the single-dimensional world is a line. No matter how you decorate it, it would not look beautiful. The two-dimensional world is a plane, a surface on which we could draw many beautiful pictures, as it has infinite times more beauty than that of the single-dimensional world. And, the three-dimensional space, as the name suggests, is infinitely times more beautiful than the two-dimensional world. The same applies to the higher dimensions. The world which is infinitely times more beautiful than our current three-dimensional world is called "Heaven" in any religion. But because of the different levels of dimensions, there are different levels of heavens.

In Buddhism, various systematic levels have been described–for example, the heavens of Mahabrahmana, Trayastrimsa, Tsuti, Nirmaarati, Parinirmita-vasavartin; the Sound Hearers and the pratyekabuddhas; and the Ten Grounds of Bodhisattva. How does Daoism describe the different levels? I have mentioned before, the Dao De Jing reads, "When Dao is lost, there is virtue (De, 德) left; when De is lost, there is humanity (Ren, 仁); when humanity is lost, there is justice (Yi, 义); when justice is lost, there is etiquette (Li, 礼); when etiquette is lost, there is benefit (Li, 利)." How does this degeneration come about? Dao is in the Nth dimension (N approaches infinity); when it is lost, the (N-1) th dimension appears. De covers the dimensions from the (N-1)th dimension to the fourth dimension. De is also an indication of the level of freedom and is described in different dimensions. The degeneration from Dao to De could be regarded as a drop in dimensions–for example, from the fourth dimension to the third dimension. In the three-dimensional world, love is the great energy, and it could be described using the word Ren. After De is lost, there is Ren. Ren (仁), a word made up of the word Man (

人) and the word Two (二), contains the meaning of two men, and also that, of these two men, one is in the usual form, which is the form of particles, and the other is invisible, being in the form of waves. This is a very precise description of life situations in the Dao De Jing, and in the Daoist wisdom system.

I have mentioned before that the Christian heart method focuses on ridding all the in-between levels of dimensions, as we human beings often cling to those levels. This approach is quite similar to that advocated in Chan, Zen Buddhism–namely, that when you are void of any form, you have the possibility to attain wisdom. As the Buddha said in the Diamond Sutra, "If anyone should think that I can be seen among forms, or that I can be sought among sounds, that person is on the wrong path." In Christianity, the worship of idols is the worship of Satan. These two religions share the same view on this. From this we can see that there are commonalities in the descriptions of life among different religions and wisdoms. Despite the differences in the methods of description, the essence of their descriptions are highly consistent, and they could verify each other.

II. The Phenomenon and Essence of Life – Projection and Projection Source

I mentioned before that the origin of life comes from the distribution of high-dimensional energy. When analysing the distribution of this energy, it is very important to see clearly the information in the projection source. When analysing the initial existence of the universe, I used the

Sine Wave in my description. When a Sine Wave appears, it is described as "one thought" in Buddhism, and "Yin and Yang" in Daoism. This is the very starting point of life, and it appears in the high dimension. If someone clings to the energy relationship, the relationship will become static. Such a static energy relationship is our perception, which reflects the energy distribution of information in the projection source. In other words, it is the spectrum entanglement created by our internal energy. When this spectrum is projected into our world, in three-dimensional space, the manifestation of the energy in relation to the spectrum rendered is the origin of life. This is why I say the origin of all lives is from perception in the higher dimensions. The level of our perception determines the kind of world that will be projected.

I have also emphasised many times, one must not seek the higher dimensional space from without. One must do so from within. Because all the information we've seen in our three-dimensional world is the projection of the source from a higher dimension, the search for the true essence in the source dimension is the right approach. The only fundamental way to acquire the connection between three-dimensional information and higher dimensional space is to seek from within. During lectures, I am often asked, "Mr. Liu, can you tell which dimension I am in?" My reply has always been very simple, "Your dimension can be judged by the environment you are in. If the environment and the people around you are all good, you are in a good dimension. If the situation is not so good, the projection source of yours couldn't be too good." In reality, if you are not satisfied with the situation you are in, the one method to rectify the situation is to seek internally the imperfection, as all reasons point to the internal imperfection. Understanding this concept will guide us to seek inwardly for our growth and improvement. All achievements are the result of an inward approach.

Due to their attachment to three-dimensional perception, human beings are restricted in their understanding of the essence of life. Human beings persistently hold the view that time is a constant element and will not change. Within such a framework of understanding, one cannot have a breakthrough in their perception and understanding. In other words, they cannot establish the link between themselves and the projection source, and they have a great fear of death. Actually, the fear for death is the gravest fear for beings in the three-dimensional world. The origin of the fear is a lack of understanding of what death is. They do not understand that death does not mean that energy scatters and vanishes. The energy, aka "soul", from the projection source cannot die, and cannot vanish, because in the fourth-dimensional world, time is a variant element. One can travel to any point of time in the past and the future. The projection source is the real origin of life. With this understanding, one truly transcends the fear of death.

When one has the correct understanding of the simple truth of life and death, they enter a totally different status in life. At the moment of their enlightenment, they will have lived out the true value of life, or, should I put it that they will have lived out the true value of their life. If they are fearful of death, all their behaviour in their life will be discounted and unfulfilled. This is because they will always be in fear of the coming of the last moment in their life, and they wouldn't understand that the essence of life is that it never ends. When we live, it's like we are all experiencing a life exam. We will have to hand in the paper eventually. Those who do not understand life's essence always want to extend the length of the exam period, yet they neglect the quality of life during the exam. Some will be terminally ill, enduring extended torture before death in a hospital bed. If this is the case, their energy would decrease, and they would be in a state of "being alive but worse than being dead". If such a situation continues, and the energy continues to decrease, the energy in their consciousness will also decrease dramatically. Such a situation is the total opposite of what a meaningful life should be. Therefore, I consider this situation totally meaningless, even if the life is prolonged. Those who have become enlightened with the true meaning of life wouldn't focus on the length of the lifespan. As we know, students can hand in their answer sheet early during an exam.

As we said before, the projected images and projection source determine all life phenomena. When we truly understand this, we understand that all depends on how we deal with the information in the projection source, and how we perceive the projection source itself. This projection source perception, referred to as "karma" in Buddhism, has a similar term in Christianity – "original sin." All information in the projection source is perception, and all perceptions are, actually, obstacles to our full and complete enlightenment. These obstacles, as projected images, appear in our lives, and can be used by us to discover our internal and original obstacles. Only by transcending them or overcoming them, are we able to walk on the path of perfect and full enlightenment, the path to "eliminate karma".

III. The Meaning of Life – To Improve the Dimension of Consciousness Energy (the Level of Freedom)

In Confucianism, there is an important classic scripture, the Great Learning, which says, "The way of the Great Learning is to illustrate illustrious virtue." De is the level of freedom. Then, what does it mean to illustrate virtue? To illustrate virtue is the highest level of freedom. The illustrious virtue, actually, is the Dao. To illustrate means to continuously surpass one's perception and ignorance, so as to improve the level of freedom, to achieve the ultimate level of illustrious virtue. That is the level of Dao, of ultimate wisdom, the level of the Nth dimension.

When explaining his view of the purpose of life, Mr. Inamori Kazuo from Japan said, "My wish, for when the end-of-life approaches, is to have raised my spirit into something even just a little more pure than it was at the time of my birth." What does this mean? We know that the soul belongs to high-dimensional space and is what I refer to as high-dimension consciousness energy. The level of the soul refers to the level of dimension of our internal energy. Mr. Inamori Kazuo founded two companies which became Top 500 companies, and he salvaged Japan Airlines. He also invented the Amoeba operating methods, and established Seiwajyuku, a private management school. With these great achievements in life, he didn't make any reference to them when talking about the purpose of life. He merely said the aforementioned line. Why? Because he had truly awakened to the true meaning of life. He understood that a life is not made great merely because of those achievements. Those achievements are the expressions of what he had achieved internally. Such internal achievements, when projected in our reality, were deemed successful by us. Therefore, it is the internal improvement in us that brings about success, rather than the success in our reality world that brings about our internal improvement.

Everyone has a different opinion of the purpose of life, based on their standing point. In reality, how could each person practice and improve their level of consciousness energy? There is a famous stanza in Chinese Zen Buddhism which describes the three levels of perception. It reads like this. 1. Seeing mountains as mountains and seeing rivers as rivers. 2. Seeing mountains not as mountains and seeing rivers not as rivers. 3. Seeing mountains once again as mountains and seeing rivers once again as rivers.

While still in the three-dimensional world, and while we haven't entered the enlightened life situations, we see all things in the world related to us as they are, and we can engage with them. At this stage, we are "seeing mountains as mountains, and seeing rivers as rivers." However, when we find ourselves helpless in a passive mode in our life, and in our destiny, we are likely to become a slave to something we like or have become attached to–for example, money, or feelings. In such a lower-dimensional world, we cannot understand the essential meaning of those matters based on superficial phenomena alone. When we've improved, when we've achieved a certain level of enlightenment, we learn that those things we had pursued in the three-dimensional world were meaningless. Just like, in our eyes, the efforts of ants are meaningless. At this stage, we are "seeing mountains not as mountains, and seeing rivers not as rivers."

When we've understood the meaning of life and have improved the level of freedom–the level of consciousness energy–we've also understood that all the things we've encountered in the three-dimensional world are the projection of our internal perceptions. All the obstacles we've encountered are clues for us to observe and to learn the true and original obstacles. At this stage, we are "seeing mountains again as mountains, and seeing rivers again as rivers." This demonstrates that we've understood the internal connections among all things that are happening to us. We would understand that all things happening to us in our lives are the projections of our perceptions, perceptions which are obstacles to our understanding. When we realize that they are the obstacles, we'd be able to focus on them. The uniting of outer projections with inner perceptions is why we say, at this stage, that we are "seeing mountains again as mountains, and seeing rivers again as rivers."

In Buddhism, the description is much easier, as in the teachings, it is said, "Affliction is Bodhi." If you are able to turn your affliction into wisdom, you would be regarded as an Arahat. This means that, when a single affliction arises in your mind, you would be able to detect it, and could use your wisdom to overcome that affliction. To conquer your afflictions is to gain wisdom. Whoever does not allow anything else to cause affliction is a true Arahat.

A Bodhisattva is someone who takes on others' afflictions and tries to conquer them. The afflictions of others become their reason for gaining wisdom and enlightenment. A Bodhisattva has endless number of reasons more than an Arahat for gaining wisdom, and, therefore, his level of wisdom is much higher than that of an Arahat. When we use the term, to generate the "Bodhi mind" or "bodhicitta", we mean Bodhisattvas who have made a great vow to solve the problems and afflictions of other beings and take them as their own goal for their own practice and perfection. In doing so, they would be able to reach the maximum level of freedom–that is, the Nth-dimensional perfection.

IV. The Worldly Heart Method – Faith, Vow, Practice and Attainment

Here, I need to introduce one very important concept, that is, how can we, in our three-dimensional world, cultivate and improve the level of freedom of our internal consciousness energy. The method involved is called the Worldly Heart Method, and it has four aspects: Faith, Vow, Action and Attainment.

What does "Faith" involve? All different systems have their own referent for it. In Buddhism, it is faith in the Buddha, and in Daoism, in the Dao. In Christianity, it is in God. And the ultimate faith points to the Nth-dimensional wisdom (N approaches infinity).

In essence, there is no difference between the 0th dimension and the Nth dimension. In other words, the 0th dimension contains all the information of the entire universe, and the connections among the information, and all the wisdom in the universe. We must have such faith that we are all intrinsically self-sufficient. This is true faith. When we truly return to our own high-dimensional space, or, when we truly return to our own 0th dimension, we would be able to experience the situation where we are intrinsically self-sufficient.

Therefore, faith is the number one essence of the Worldly Heart Method. If you don't believe you are intrinsically self-sufficient, you won't be able to realize your internal perfection, as "Faith is the source of Dao, and is the mother of all virtues". Such faith is the true faith. All descriptions are made for the fulfilment of such faith. Such faith, when at its top level, is in unity with the entire universe. However, it is not an exaggeration of pride. With such faith, you would not be belittling yourself, as you would be driven by your pursuit of improvement. With such faith, you would not be too proud, as you would know all beings in the universe as intrinsically self-sufficient, and you would have the mentality of equality and great harmony.

But having the true faith is not enough. One must also, as the second step, make a great vow. What is a vow? It is a target, something we must have as a goal for our internal improvement.

Have we not all experienced things when we were little that either terrified or extremely puzzled us? Then, when we grew up and looked back at those things, they were so trivial we often laughed at our own naivety. We could do this because we had grown up. This is also true for mountain climbing. In our first attempts, we are worried even by the height of a small mountain. However, after conquering that, and after climbing onto the top of an even higher mountain, the fear we had at the foot of the small mountain seems nothing, even laughable. The great poet Du Fu from the Tang dynasty had written his famous verse, "One day I'll climb to the top of a summit, and all mountains around me will look so trivial." If, on the contrary, we were not brave enough to climb even a small hill, we would not even start the journey. And even if we did start climbing, we might be deterred by our own negative thoughts and become tired very easily. Only when we set a clear goal to climb and conquer the mountain will we act swiftly and with great mind power. Such is the power of a vow, that it enables us to climb the mountain with ease, and even with great elegance. This is the importance of a vow. With a great vow and the power generated by it, it would be hard for one not to succeed. With a great vow, we would have more chances of succeeding. There is a saying that, to a person who has a great vow, there is no difficult thing. If we are terrified when faced with a serious matter in life, and cannot overcome our fear, that would only prove we haven't been through enough–haven't been challenged by enough–to have made a strong vow. Making a great vow, therefore, is one of the critical steps in life.

In the Diamond Sutra, we read that Sariputra asked the Buddha a question, "In what should a virtuous man or a virtuous woman abide in, and how should they subdue their minds?" Buddha Sakyamuni answered, "For a virtuous man or a virtuous woman who has already generated the mind of Anuttara-samyak-sambodhi, they should abide as such, and

165

should subjugate their minds as such." This vow–for the attainment of complete, unsurpassed, and perfect enlightenment–is also known as the wisdom of the Nth-dimensional world. In Christian theology, it is called "God be with them." This is a truly great vow, to return to the Kingdom of God, as that Kingdom is the Nth-dimensional space. In Confucianism, we have learned that "the way of the Great Learning is to illustrate illustrious virtue." The illustrious virtue is the wisdom in the Nth-dimensional world (N approaches infinity). In Daoism, we read, "Heaven and man integrated as one". This also means that, when we reach the Nth-dimensional world (N approaches infinity), we have reached the summit of all wisdom. Therefore, all great vows point to the highest level of wisdom. In our lives, in our pursuit of wisdom and spiritual improvement, we must not attach to any level that is below the Nth dimension. However, at the same time, we must not neglect any energies and appearances, nor be superstitious about any of them. We must take them as our reinforcing conditions, as they are all ladders for us to improve, and to surpass our limited perceptions and understandings.

After making a vow, the next step is to practice, and to start actions. Whoever intends to get to the top of a mountain, must not stand at the bottom and do nothing. They must, gazing high with their eyes, set out from below with their feet. Furthermore, I'd like to emphasize, they must have "heart actions."

Why do I emphasize "heart actions"? All actions stem from the heart, or heart/mind. If we couldn't make improvements in the projection source, and we only worked on the projected images, we could not climb to the top of the mountain in our heart. Therefore, we must take "heart actions", by using "heart methods." How can we apply the heart methods in the three-dimensional world? Very simply. First, we must observe and discern. All things happening to us are related to our internal spiritual growth, and to our internal perceptions. Therefore, we must observe and discern.

To observe and discern is to identify the issue. When we identify the issue, we must understand it, and the precondition for doing that is to reflect upon ourselves. The purpose of identifying the issue is to understand what kind of perception and understanding is behind that issue, as all understanding is from within, not from without. If we try to find the reason from without, this process will not help us in our improvement. Only when we seek inwardly, can we find the issue, and it can help us improve. Only after such inward reflection, enabling us to understand the cause of the issue, could we transcend our wrong understanding, and begin to "eliminate karma". At the very moment we transcend our wrong understanding, we would feel our improvement, and we could establish the connection with the high-dimensional space. At that very moment, we would feel the great joy, like the "Dharma joy" described in Buddhism. Those who have not experienced this cannot understand that this is more valuable than any worldly joy and happiness.

Lives linked up by a chain of such incidents of Dharma joy would be relaxed, happy, and full of creativity. But always, the purpose of life depends on the situation of the current moment. All practices and cultivations are for the current moment, through which alone the action of the heart enables us to make connection with high-dimensional energy.

There is another important step for the "heart action"–i.e., to constantly make connections with the internal high-dimensional wisdom. Meditation, reciting mantras and sutras, praying, Yoga practices, and other inwardly directed practices, are all kinds of "heart methods". They are fundamental ways of making connections with the internal high-dimensional wisdom. If we could not engage our internal actions, and we only dwelt at the surface, that would only be low-dimensional practice, and could not solve essential problems. Therefore, the "heart methods" and the "heart actions" are the practices of the higher dimension.

To do such practices, one must be equipped with high-dimensional conditions. How could we create the high-dimensional conditions in our three-dimensional space? There are five aspects.

First, jing, (净) as in purity. When we have purity internally, we are thoroughly able to make connections with the high-dimensional space.

Second, jing (静), as in tranquillity. Only when the water in a lake is tranquil are, we able to see the bottom of the lake; and how it reflects the sun, the moon and the stars. We also need tranquillity in our heart.

Third, jing (敬), as in respect. When we understand that the wisdom in the Nth-dimensional world is endless times more powerful than that in our three-dimensional world, such empowered wisdom becomes our guide to lead us to improvement. We must unconditionally allow ourselves to be subdued by such power in order to transcend all self-attachment and Dharma-attachment. Respect is a must in this regard.

Fourth, jing (镜), as in mirror. If we imagine that we are in the centre of a ball-shaped mirror, in every direction we looked, we would see the image of our self. This helps us to understand how all external things are the projection of our internal thoughts. There is no one in the universe separate from you.

Fifth, jing (境), as in environment and the level of achievement. When we are ignorant and lost, we need to create a path or an environment to lead us to long-term progress. For example, when we, as like-minded practitioners, come together for a retreat or a workshop in a certain place, we create a wholesome human environment. We have left the chaos and entanglements of the city, and have created an optimal environment for our cultivation. Therefore, environment is very important for us. At the same time, we must accurately observe the level of our cultivation and improvement if we are to achieve appropriate solutions for our issues. For example, if we are a first grader in primary school, and we have been given a high school level problem, we wouldn't benefit from the exercise. Thus, the environment and the level of cultivation are equally important in practice, as we know best what can and cannot be achieved at our level and in our environment.

These five aspects are the pre-conditions of the consciousness status necessary for us to enter the high-dimensional space.

After talking about faith, vow, and action, the last aspect is attainment. Attainment is a verified achievement of the truth. Such verification has one pre-condition: to face your true self with your true heart. Only by doing so, can you truly understand your internal perception. If, however, you guard yourself with worldly knowledge, there will be an obstacle between your internal perception and the true image, but an obstacle that you cannot see. When you can face your true self, this reality will present to you your best verification. When you decide with your true instinct what you want to do, and you succeed in doing it, you have thereby become intrinsically self-sufficient. If you failed, such failure could help you identify the obstacle to your understandings, and, next time, you'd be more likely to succeed, and able to overcome your obstacle. We all know another saying, "Failure is the mother of success." With the pre-condition of a true heart, one can confidently pursue the path of Faith, Vow, Action and Attainment.

Each of the processes of Faith, Vow, Action and Attainment can help us verify that we are all intrinsically self-sufficient. Each verification gives us tremendous faith. In carrying out the cultivation process by using the worldly heart methods, we should start with small things which are not very consequential. By applying our true heart in the practice, we can gradually build up our faith.

On the contrary, if we do not carry out the cultivation process by using the worldly heart methods, we would be puzzled, and we could not even set the correct path of our lives, let alone take any concrete steps on it. Therefore, the worldly heart methods show us the true and fundamental meaning of life, and help us improve the level of freedom of consciousness energy in our real world. Of course, there are many other methods one could take up, as there are many ways described in many different wisdoms and religions. But for those who have not renounced the mundane world in pursuit of life-long cultivation, this worldly heart method is the way to practice.

TESTIMONY

by Liu Feng

Open Your Inner High-Dimensional Wisdom ——

Entering the Great Ease of Perfection in Life

May 2020

Human beings have been exploring the meaning of life ever since human civilization started. For the past 2,500 years, various religions have been doing their share in the explorations. The New Age Movement which started several decades ago has many examples of recent searches. Countless number of description systems have been found to define the meaning of life. When one takes a position in a space which is limited in its dimension, one only see endless differences and discriminations. However, if one sees from a holistic perspective, the entire universe is one entity, and one sees projections of all possibilities.

In the past thirty years, with the comprehensive lift of energy of space and time, Xin Neng Yuan (Heart Energy Affinity) starts to present itself gradually. The connection of energies within a life takes the form of esoteric to exoteric, and then from invisible to visible. Seeking

Commonality and Respecting Differences is the basic principle for entering the secular world — by respecting the reasonableness of all existence in terms of their space and time, because the fundamental significance of our diversified and multifaceted lives is their common ultimate pursuits. The ultimate purpose of all description systems is the sole truth. Each of the descriptions, when faced with the ultimate truth, would have its unique meaning, as well as its relative restriction. Only when one is not restricted by any single description system would one be able to truly and comprehensively embrace and accept all description systems and turn each encounter in life into a supportive condition through one's inner development, and to be industrious in every moment in life for one's self cultivation in this multicultural world. With such a mentality one would be able to bury the hatchet, to turn afflictions into Bodhi, and all sounds into a harmonious symphony.

This book uses the scientific context and builds an intertwined network system of all wisdoms. By using the principle of simplicity, it distils the key terms and core logical relations. It does not belong to a person, an organization, an independent interest body, a religious entity or a governmental institute. It is the common intellectual wealth of mankind, an internal bridge which connects each entity and the organization, a hub connecting all wisdom systems in our human society; and is the shared basic frequency in the harmonious symphony of multiculturalism in our society.

I am grateful to the inner "self" for creating this opportunity, the yuan, to meet with you through the form of this book. Those who benefit the most will be those who participate.

This is the common experience shared by practitioners of Xin Neng Yuan.

Mr. Liu Feng

TESTIMONY

by Mr. Yisheng Zhao

The Symphony of High Dimensional Wisdoms

More than ten years ago, I saw Mr. Liu Feng's lectures on High Dimensional Wisdoms. His teachings covered the Projection Theory, Holographic Theory, Quantum Theory, and Negative Entropy Theory, which were not unfamiliar to me, as I had heard about them from Mr. Yuting Pan's residence in Shanghai in the 1980s. However, my main focus then was on Buddhism and I Ching, so I did not pursue them.

In 2019, I came across a video of Mr. Liu Feng lecturing on "Infinite Light and Infinite Life", and it struck a chord in my heart. I felt that lecture was specifically addressed to me. His meaningful words were a sound theoretical summary of what I had been practicing over the past 20 years. I went on and explored more of his teachings, and gained more understanding of the High Dimensional Wisdom system.

A great opportunity came up in October 2019 and it was with great excitement that I attended the Melbourne Forum in which Mr. Liu was one of the guest speakers. Through the introduction by Ms Shang Liu, I was very lucky to have the opportunity to speak in detail with Mr. Liu Feng. Once

175

again, I was greatly touched by Mr. Liu's knowledge, and I benefited a lot.

Several years ago, Mr. Liu had given a series of lectures online, and the contents had been transcribed and published in China. After the Forum held last year, a group of devoted like-minded people decided to translate the book Open Up the Higher Dimensional Wisdoms into English for the benefit of English readers who might be interested in Mr. Liu's teachings.

I was one of them who strongly advocated the publishing of this book, as I have benefited personally from Mr. Liu's teachings. He had said, "Classic scriptures of different religions come from the higher dimensions", and that, "the Pure Land practice of reciting the name of Buddha Amitabha is a way to ensure connection with the higher dimensions." Being a practicing Buddhist, I understand that, if it were not for his 30 years of experience, he could not have said such great truth. Without my two decades of practice, I could not understand what he had meant in these lines.

There are numerous sayings in Mr. Liu's teachings, and I am sure all will resonate with Mr. Liu in their own capabilities. Through modern scientific context, and through simple language, Mr. Liu discusses the principle of ultimate simplicity, seeking commonality and respecting difference, theory of high dimensional practices, comprehension and cultivation in one, and also on the oscillation of objects of the same frequency, all of which the reader will be able to find in this book.

Ever since the Forum, I have become a devoted fan of Mr. Liu, and I talk about him with every person I meet, and discuss High Dimensional Wisdoms on every possible occasion. Some of my friends have already been influenced by me, and have been sharing Mr. Liu's teachings with their friends.

The year 2020 will be an important year for Mr. Liu's High Dimensional Wisdoms as this book has now been translated into English, and will be published. The title is The Symphony of High Dimensional Wisdoms. This is a milestone for Mr. Liu as his High Dimensional Wisdoms theory will be entering the English-speaking world.

The translator of this book, Mr. Bo Ai, is a Melbourne-based interpreter and translator. During the time he was translating this book, a group of us participated in a weekly online discussion in which Mr. Ai and Mr. Liu were present. Detailed questions were asked and answered. Further elaboration by Mr. Liu assisted the comprehension and the choice of words in the translation. I wish this book to be a success, and more and more people will have the opportunity to benefit from Mr. Liu's teachings.

Yisheng Zhao,

Principal,

Perth I Ching Academy

26 April 2020

TESTIMONY

by Pei Guo

30 May 2020

In the course of my life, I try to express life, emotion and love with fashion art - Haute Couture.

I pursue "truth" and think that everything beautiful starts from "truth"; I pursue the inner "state" and the authentic "spirit".

I firmly believe in the true meaning of "internalization of the external scene, externalization of the internal state", and I believe that my works can also purify people's hearts and influence human nature.

I regard every piece of my work as a memory left to this era. That is not a passing fad; it will transcend life and become eternal.

In this world full of materialism, many people lose their way, do not understand the meaning of life, let alone the value of life.

Sometimes I felt lonely. When I met Mr. Liu Feng, his research on the high-dimensional wisdom of the universe suddenly penetrated my heart and made my life full of strength. I was at ease in my life, believing in perfection, and no longer lonely. Do appreciate this opportunity to meet Mr. Liu Feng in your life.

Guo Pei

The first and only Chinese couture designer approved around the world.

30 May 2020

Mr. Liu Feng

TESTIMONY

by Songlin Liu

12 May 2020

I have been working in corporate training and traditional Chinese cultural training for over 10 years' time, and have known Mr. Liu Feng for almost 10 years. In recent years, I have been fortunate enough to work alongside Mr. Liu Feng for a period of time. The awareness dimension, level, disposition and breadth of Mr. Liu Feng have all had a profound impact on my life. What is particularly precious to individuals and groups alike is the important direction provided by Mr. Liu Feng in his 30 years of multicultural system compilation in the realm of inner growth groups. To me, the meaning of life is continuous progress and improvement. This book has afforded me tremendous help in the dimension of how scientific context can uplift awareness energy, and I will keep on studying it.

Songlin Liu

Founder of Bene Wellness

Initiator of Holistic Wellness International Forum with Holistic Center Networks

TESTIMONY

by Shugong Fang

14 May 2020

I made Mr. Liu Feng's acquaintance ten years ago, and we co-founded the "Shi-Fang-Yuan" elderly mental care charity organisation, providing mental care services for 40 million severely ill, terminal-stage elderly in China. We have expanded to 87 cities with 143 organisations and over 200 thousand volunteer services delivered. Many have asked me why there have been so many volunteers participating? I particularly like to share what was said by Mr. Liu Feng: "The elderly are the projection of awareness for the companions, and the fundamental meaning of serving the elderly lies within the uplifting of awareness energy for each companion, realising the value and purpose of their own lives whilst accompanying a process of life, and that is a self-education on life." We have seen that every life needs care and compassion, and we have seen every life moving towards satisfaction. Therefore, we do not analyse, nor do we judge or define. What we do is only to love and be there. Mr. Liu Feng's theory system has made an impact on the life satisfaction of thousands of people. I look forward to the publication of the English version of the book "Tapping into Higher-Dimension Wisdom". I believe it will connect with more people who are meant to be, and awaken the satisfaction originating from life.

Shugong Fang

Director, Beijing Shi-Fang-Yuan Elderly Mental Care Centre

Secretary-General of the Beijing Shi-Fang-Yuan Charity Foundation

Executive Director of China Life Care Association.

TESTIMONY

by Liwei Wang

On Behalf of All Volunteers

Since the breakout of the COVID-19 pandemic in the beginning of 2020, we have seen the relationship between the community with a shared future for mankind and each person, and that no single nation, people, or individual can remain unaffected in this day and age.

With scientific advancements, the development of internet technology, big data, and artificial intelligence has brought us closer together, and made us ever more connected. With this as the backdrop, we would not be able to solve problems at their root causes should we elect to view them from a regional and not a global perspective.

The core of the community with a shared future for mankind, then, is the harmonious symphony of a multitude of cultures. All human conflicts have been rooted in religious differences. History has shown through millennia that one religion, however strong, has not been able to completely dominate another, for example Buddhism and Christianity. Laws of nature have also told us that any single being cannot survive and thrive continuously, just like any single agricultural produce cannot exist on its own. There has to be a different energy there to strike a balance, and thus only a diverse eco-system can develop sustainably. This is an objective law.

The key to the harmonious symphony of a multitude of cultures is this – pursuing commonness whilst respecting differences, completely respecting the legitimacy of a culture in its time and its place, seeking the common components of every culture. If humanity be the whole, seeing things through a singular perspective would be as if the arms stated that they are more important than the legs. If they cut the legs off, humanity would be unable to take a single step.

The biggest question in today's world is not that of the pandemic, nor that of the well-being of career, or that of life or death, or that of the impact of scientific advancements on life. It is one of how we correctly perceive life. Who are we? How have we come into this world? What is the meaning of our lives? Where are we going?

Mr. Liu Feng has spent 30 years seeking the common components in all of the wisdom systems he has had the fortune to come into contact with, and forming this wisdom system of the fundamental principles of the universe. For this wisdom system, Mr. Liu Feng has not invented any peculiar names or terminologies, but has only borrowed from the universal and simplest scientific terms and logics, for the purpose of revealing the meaning of life to each being from the perspective of now.

TESTIMONY

by Dr. Xiaoming Cheng

30/05/2020, Boston, USA

Fall is the most beautiful season in New Hampshire. I was taking a stroll with Mr. Liu Feng along the narrow path naturally formed in between the mountains, appreciating the charm of nature. Wherever he showed up, he was always appearing to be in a state close to nature. What impressed me the most were his eyes, especially when he was gazing. The pureness at the bottom of the heart is combined together with a bright look, as if shining in the light of wisdom.

"The simplest principles of the universe that you promote truly accurately sum up the commonness of all beings in the three-dimension world. After necessity increases the level of freedom of the inner awareness energy, not only is your horizon broadened, but you also break free from the knowledge and understanding in your vicinity. Yours is an unprecedented pathway towards improving insight and understanding wisdom." I couldn't help commenting.

We casually walked on the road covered by red leaves, reflecting the image of forest through the setting sun in the evening. Fresh air. Experiencing the complete unification with nature. My words seemed to have stirred up his thoughts within. He did not think, but merely took in a breath of the fresh air. The quietness allowed us to hear our own blood flowing, stepping on the falling leaves. He responded: in the last thirty years, I have been trying to figure out the conflict of humanity caused by the differences between multiple cultures in the world, which is never ending. In today's world of continuous development of human civilisation, what humanity needs to do is to tolerate various cultures, and compose a symphony of harmonious co-existence. And to do that is to understand the commonness of all human cultures.

Mr. Liu Feng went on sharing: and so, our fear of death in the three-dimension world would be completely transcended, which is the key to true life transcendence. And so, it helps us understand the state of balance of energy returning to nature. It is the Way, and the Way governs nature.

"Right!" I immediately commented in agreement, that this is a feeling of "learning the Way in the morning pardons the sorrow of death in the evening". It is truly difficult to jump out of confusing knowledge, particularly when one is trapped at the knowledge level of the three-dimension space. Like a fish breaking out of a net.

I remember one time when I tortured myself close to insanity, with various materials flying around in my mind in Chinese, English, French and Japanese, and all sorts of essays in physiology, bio-chemistry, anatomy, and molecular medicine cramming my head, making it almost explode. All the internal anatomical structures and physiological functions appeared in my brain like a storm. So, I put down the materials at hand, sprinted out of the room, stood in the heavy snow, and looked at the silver-grey sky, facing up, allowing the chilly snowflakes to fall on my face, stinging it. Suddenly, a phrase appeared in my brain:" the greatest Way is the simplest". Instantaneously, all of the miscellaneous thoughts fell on the ground like snowflakes. The word "human" was clear as day in my mind. I was thinking, should God be looking down on the puny mortals from above, would the human understanding focused on the three-dimensional space appear laughable?

The teacher of Einstein, the father of quantum mechanics – Dr. Planck, who won the Nobel Prize of Physics in 1918, once remarked: my ultimate conclusion on my research of atoms is this – there is no such thing as matter in this world, but merely what is formed by fast vibrating quanta. With or without a form, all is but ever vibrating energy. The distinction between the two lies in the difference in vibration frequency, thus producing different matters with different ideas or forms. Those with a high vibration frequency become formless matters, for example, people's thoughts, feelings and ideas; and those with a low vibration frequency become visible matters with a form, like desks, chairs, human bodies, etc. The common property of matters is energy wave, and the minimum appearance of energy waves is the sine wave (simple harmonic wave), which embodies the nature of any wave, and the foundation of all matter existences, constituting the core of the universe.

What this book explains with the simplest principles of the universe is the common property of all matters. We know that science is the exploration and interpretation of the laws of the universe and of nature, and science is one of the ways of expressing higher-dimension wisdoms of the universe. I believe that their expression at the level of three-dimensional knowledge must be diverse. And when humans

187

explain the expression of this higher-dimension wisdom at the level of three-dimensional knowledge, they must be repeatedly making many useless arguments with knowledge of all types, due to the limits of human understanding.

What this book does, however, is exactly leading confused humans out of the confines of their barricades with the explanation approach at the level of higher-dimension wisdom, seeking commonness whilst respecting differences, knowing, understanding, and creatively selecting the best solutions at a higher level.

This book tells us about realising the purpose of life, and that we should have sufficient confidence in our internal environment to harness energy of all dimensions. That means believing in the presence of higher-dimension wisdom within. Everyone has enough internally, and the internal wisdom is N-dimensional (with N approaching infinity).

A book is written to be read, not to be a decoration of the shelves or of the room. Mr. Liu Feng's book is just like his eyes, containing no miscellaneous thoughts, nor utilitarian purposes. What can be seen are only pureness and offering.

Dr. Xiaoming Cheng

Doctor at Osher Center for Integrative Medicine, Harvard University

Epilogue

The English version of "Opening High Dimensional Wisdom Dialogues" was launched in 2019, soon after the "Traditional Chinese Culture and High-dimensional Wisdom Forum" was held in Melbourne between 1-3 November 2019. During the forum, Mr. Liu Feng was one of the main speakers. Mr. Liu shared his view on life in the context of science, and the ultimate meaning of life. The audience had the opportunity to learn his very refreshing theory about life.

In this extraordinary period on this planet, we have been given a special gift since the end of 2019, witnessing, experiencing the COVID 19 outbreak that shocked the world. This English translation is presented by those who are awakening during this historical event. We are very grateful to all those who have been connected because of this book.

Especially, we like to thank:

- All the volunteers who contributed their time in this project
- Sponsor for Bodhi Foundation for the "Traditional 0Chinese Culture and High-Dimensional Wisdoms Forum" held between 1-3 November 2019 in Melbourne
- Artist Li Shuang, who designed covers and painting illustrations in the book
- Bo Ai who translated the book from Chinese into English

Mr. Liu Feng

- Jonathan Bricklin, Maggie Mee, Haoyu Zhao, Xin Liao, Hua Li, Kathy Rabb Kittok for their English editing suggestions.
- Mr. Zhao Yisheng's editing in Chinese version
- Ding Dong's donation for the illustration drawings in the book
- Peter J. Liang for book publishing and marketing advices.
- Haoyu Zhao for project coordination.
- Thanks to Dongze, Hailing of MINDSUP for their support.
- All volunteers at the International Holographic Ecology Ltd for their contribution.

The year of 2020 is bound to be a turning point in human history. And we wish having you along the way to awakening.

International Holographic Ecology Ltd
Dec 2021

Linking diversified human wisdom systems through scientific context, and realizing harmonious coexistence of humanity and nature.

Mr. Liu Feng

Made in the USA
Monee, IL
05 March 2021